SHAKA

A LEGEND OF THE WARRIOR PRINCE

RISING

LUKE W. MOLVER & MASON O'CONNOR

Published by **Story Press Africa**, an imprint of
Jive Media Africa (South Africa) and **Catalyst Press** (USA).
Website: www.storypressafrica.com

Jive Media Africa

P O Box 22106
Mayor's Walk
3208
South Africa

Tel: +27 33 342 9380/2
Email: admin@jivemedia.co.za
Website: www.jivemedia.co.za

Catalyst Press

2941 Kelly Street
Livermore CA 94551 USA

Tel: 001-925-315-5970
Email: jlpowers@catalystpress.org
Website: www.catalystpress.org

Illustrated by: Luke W. Molver
Written by: Luke W. Molver, Mason O'Connor
Acknowledgement: This work has drawn on *Myth of Iron: Shaka in History* by Dan Wylie

Library of Congress Control Number: 2017947777

Trade Paper ISBN 978-1-946498-98-4

Trade Cloth ISBN 978-1-946498-99-1

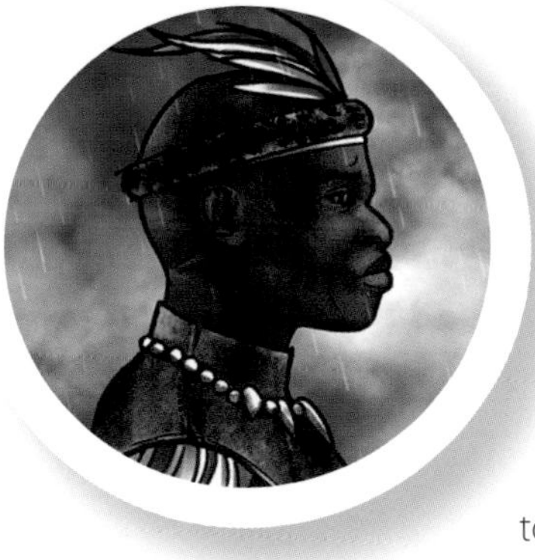

FOREWORD

It is a privilege to have been invited to write the Foreword to this imaginative and innovative presentation of the story of Shaka, the legendary founder of the Zulu Kingdom. The Cambridge Advanced Learner's Dictionary defines legends as very old "stories, not always true, that people tell about a famous event or person." As with all legends, there are numerous accounts of the story of this remarkable ruler. This version synthesizes different accounts of his birth, rejection by his father, years of exile from his people and eventual ascendance to the throne.

The legend of Shaka in the English-speaking world was founded on accounts by white travellers, traders, explorers, missionaries, historians and writers with perspectives and agendas very different from those of the Zulu people. In my work on Southern African Studies, and particularly on Southern African literature written in English, I have focused on Shakan literature; analyzed accounts by black South African and West African writers; and recent historiographic research on the use of oral history as a source of reliable historical information.

The **African Graphic Novel Series** aims to make great African stories accessible to a world-wide audience of young readers, drawing on multiple sources to ensure balanced and credible accounts.

Shaka Rising, the first book in this series, tells Shaka's story with great sensitivity and insight, accompanied by action packed graphics and interesting personal touches that highlight the strengths and weaknesses of various Nguni leaders. It brings history alive to many who would ordinarily not read standard historical accounts. The authors are to be commended for producing an interesting and engaging account of perhaps the best known African monarch in Southern Africa.

Mbongeni Z. Malaba
Professor of English Studies,
University of KwaZulu-Natal
Pietermaritzburg.

SHAKA
Son of Senzangakhona
and Nandi

THE CHARACTERS IN "SHAKA RISING"

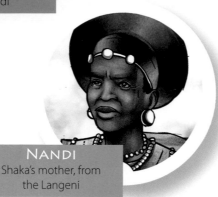

NANDI
Shaka's mother, from
the Langeni

NOMCOBA
Shaka's sister

SENZANGAKHONA
Chief of the Zulu,
Shaka's father

SIGUJANA
Shaka's half-brother,
son of Senzangakhona
and Mbhibhi

NDENGEZI
Friend of Shaka

DINGANE
Shaka's half-brother

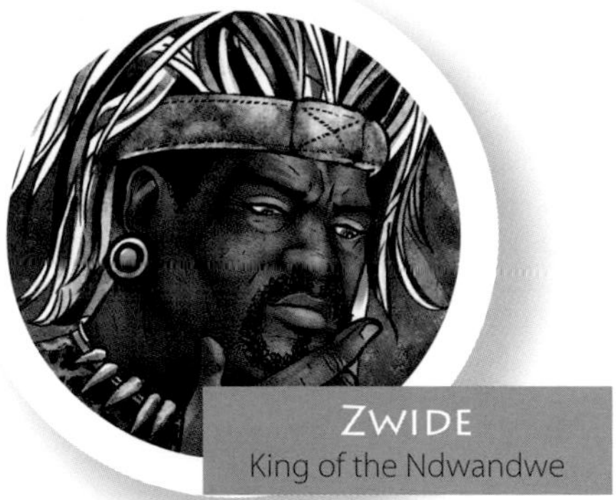

ZWIDE
King of the Ndwandwe

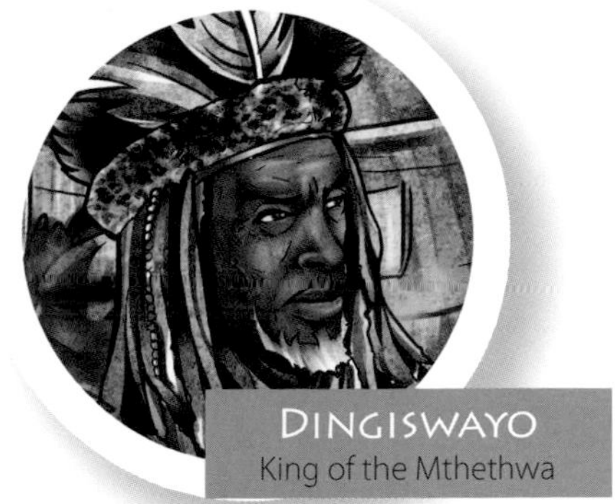

DINGISWAYO
King of the Mthethwa

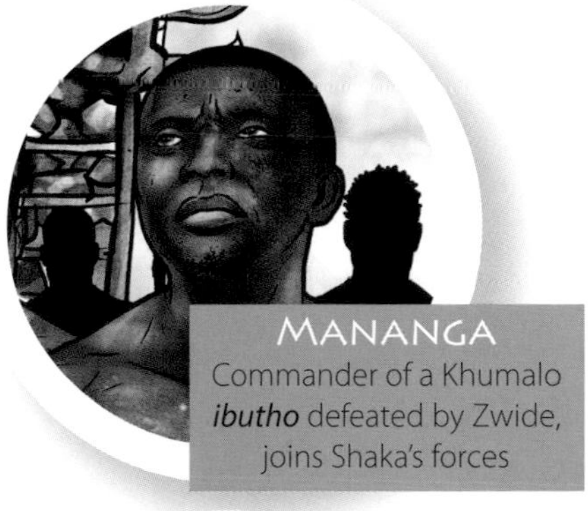

MANANGA
Commander of a Khumalo *ibutho* defeated by Zwide, joins Shaka's forces

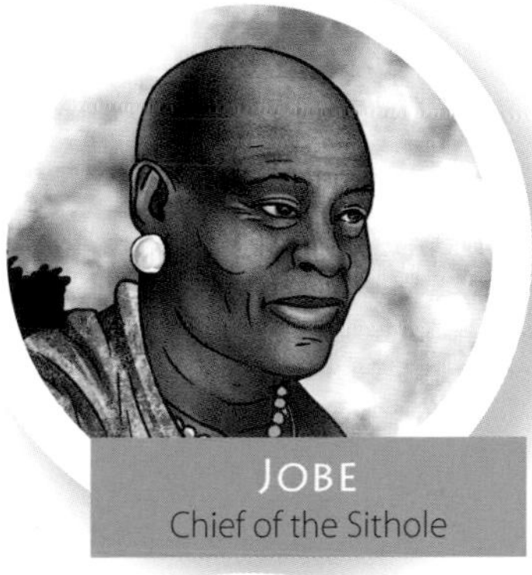

JOBE
Chief of the Sithole

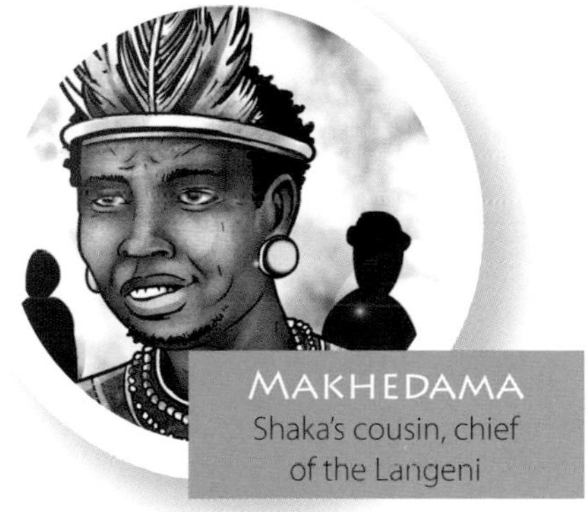

MAKHEDAMA
Shaka's cousin, chief of the Langeni

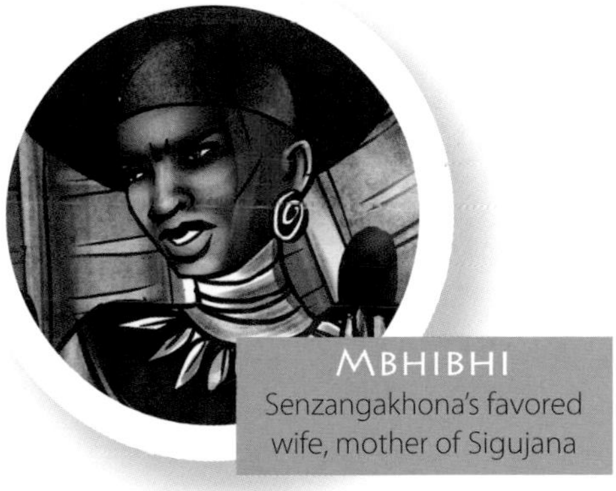

MBHIBHI
Senzangakhona's favored wife, mother of Sigujana

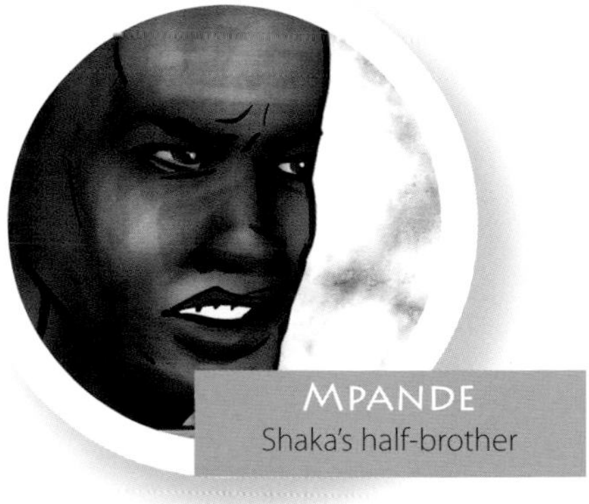

MPANDE
Shaka's half-brother

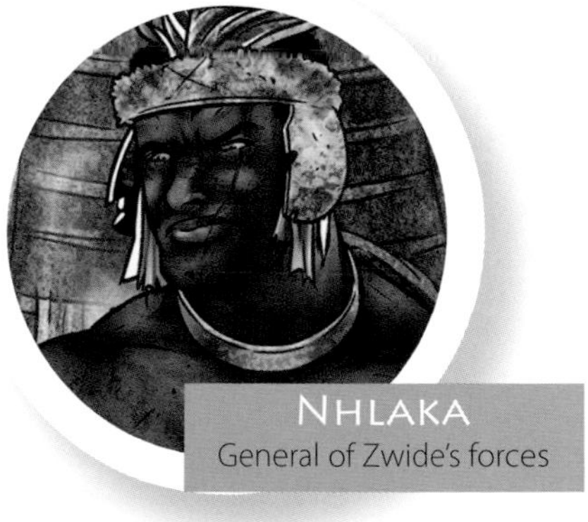

NHLAKA
General of Zwide's forces

THE WORLD OF "SHAKA RISING"

The last part of the 18th century was the time of the American Revolution, the French Revolution, and the expansion of European colonization.

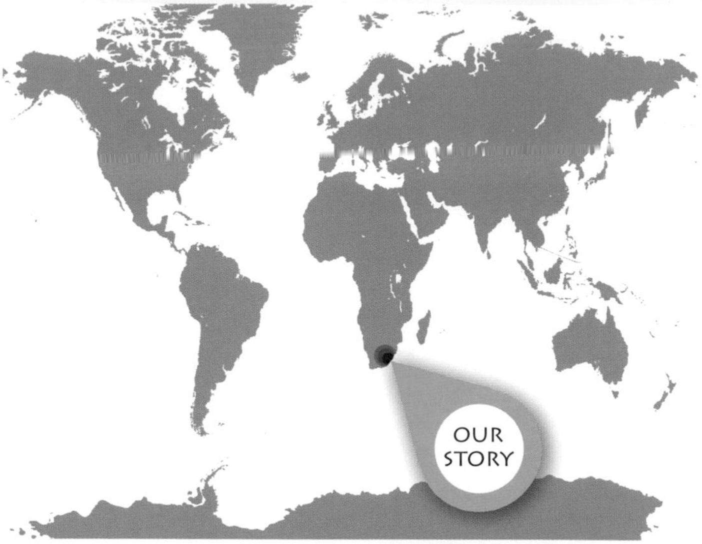
OUR STORY

This was also a time of great turmoil and bloody conflict in south-eastern Africa. The Ndwandwe kingdom, to the north of the Zulu, was expanding its power and territory, attacking neighboring clans and selling them into slavery through the port of Delagoa Bay.

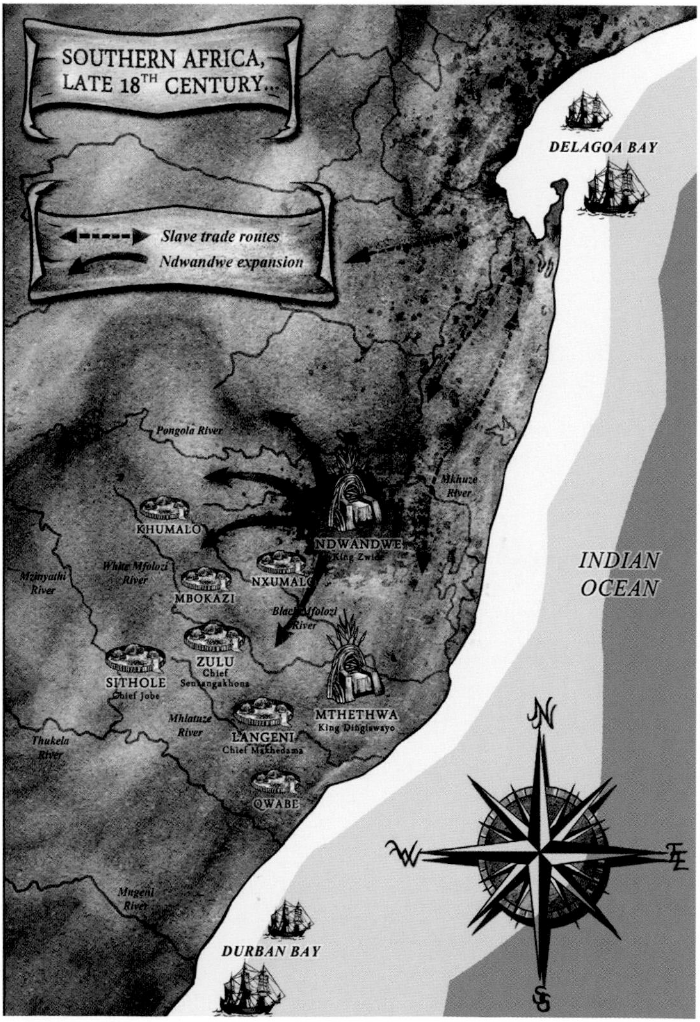
SOUTHERN AFRICA, LATE 18TH CENTURY...
Slave trade routes
Ndwandwe expansion
DELAGOA BAY
Pongola River
Mkhuze River
KHUMALO
NDWANDWE
White Mfolozi River
Mzinyathi River
NXUMALO
MBOKAZI
INDIAN OCEAN
ZULU
Chief
SITHOLE
Chief Jobe
Mhlatuze River
MTHETHWA
King Dingiswayo
Thukela River
LANGENI
Chief Makhedama
QWABE
Mngeni River
DURBAN BAY
N
W
E
S

This was the time and region into which Shaka was born, in a small clan surrounded by other chiefdoms vying for control. Through warfare, mediation, and political alliances, Shaka defeated the Ndwandwe and consolidated a new kingdom that has stood to this day.

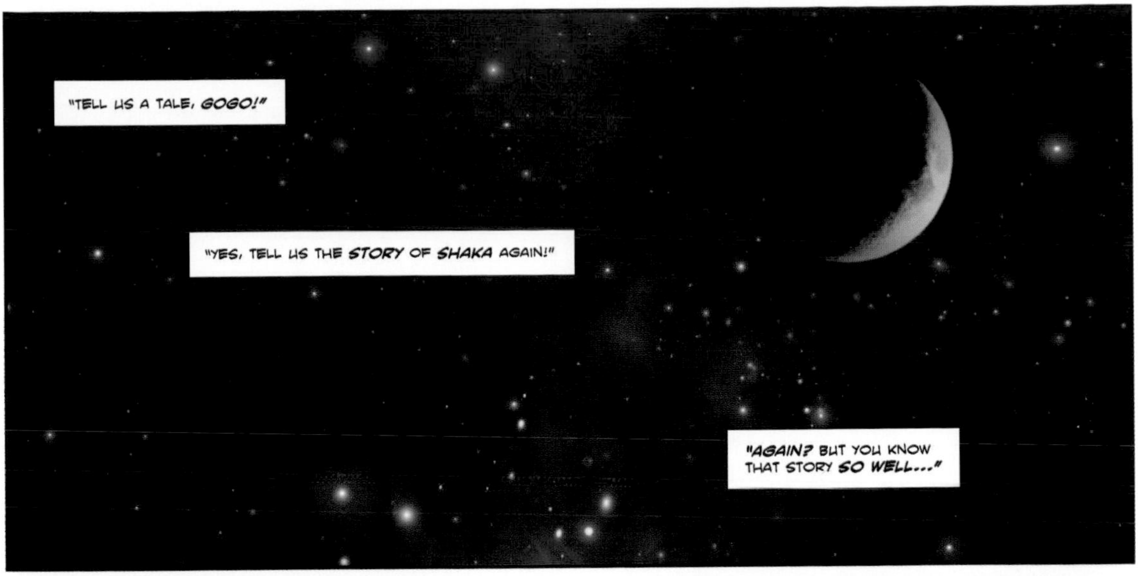
"TELL US A TALE, GOGO!"
"YES, TELL US THE STORY OF SHAKA AGAIN!"
"AGAIN? BUT YOU KNOW THAT STORY SO WELL..."

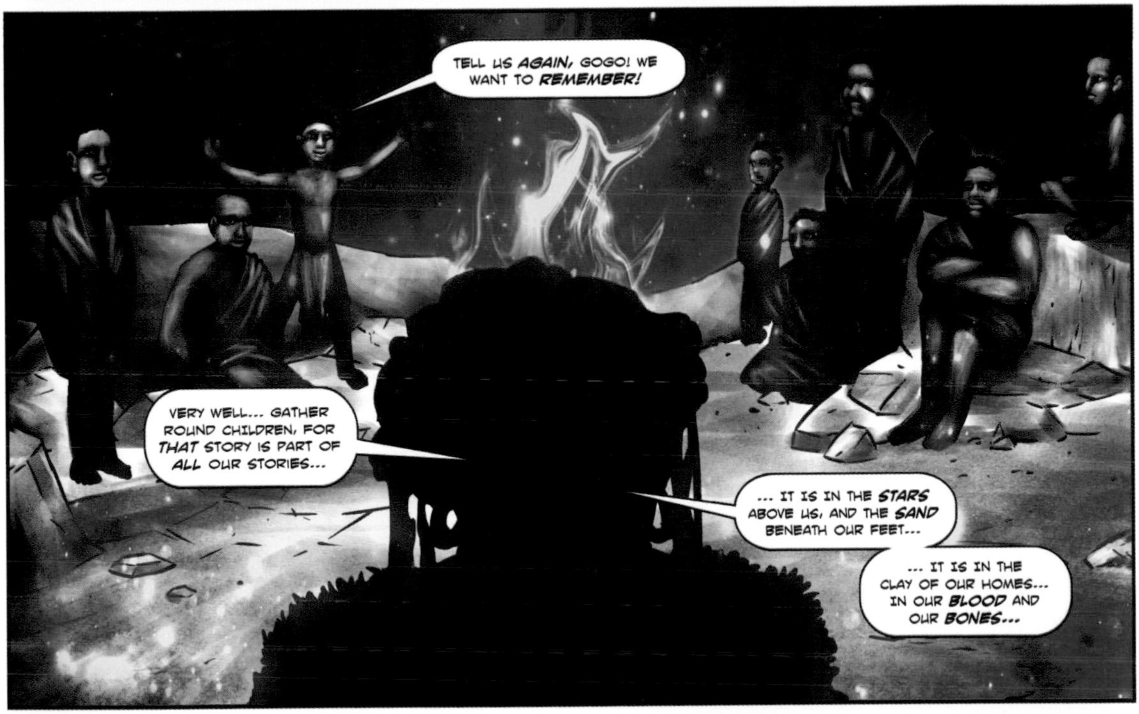
TELL US AGAIN, GOGO! WE WANT TO REMEMBER!
VERY WELL... GATHER ROUND CHILDREN, FOR THAT STORY IS PART OF ALL OUR STORIES...
... IT IS IN THE STARS ABOVE US, AND THE SAND BENEATH OUR FEET...
... IT IS IN THE CLAY OF OUR HOMES... IN OUR BLOOD AND OUR BONES...

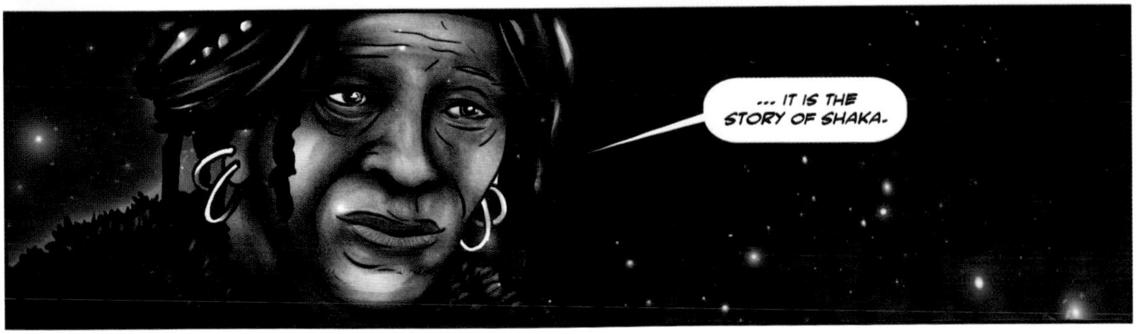
... IT IS THE STORY OF SHAKA.

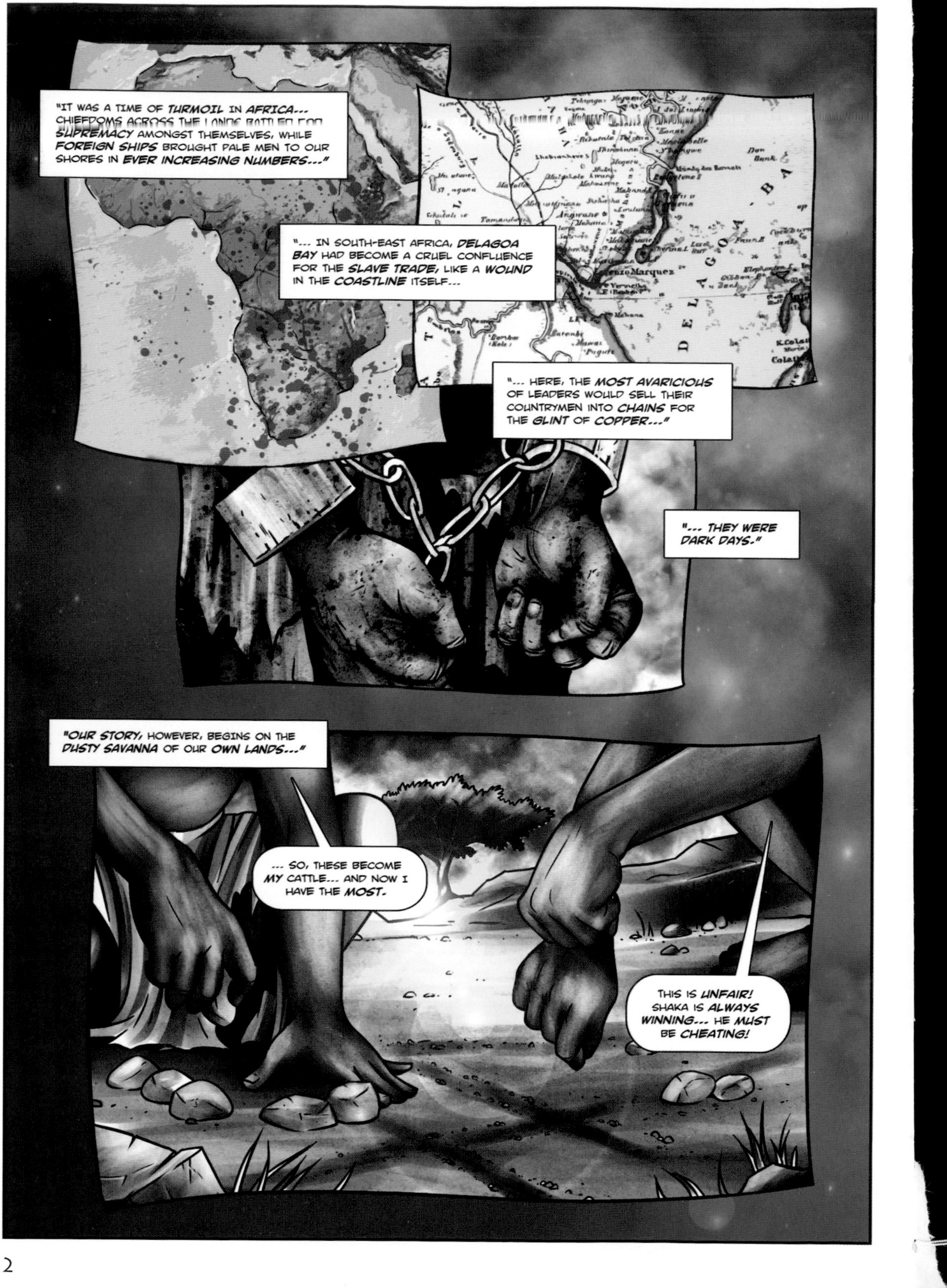
"IT WAS A TIME OF *TURMOIL* IN *AFRICA...* CHIEFDOMS ACROSS THE LANDS BATTLED FOR *SUPREMACY* AMONGST THEMSELVES, WHILE *FOREIGN SHIPS* BROUGHT PALE MEN TO OUR SHORES IN *EVER INCREASING NUMBERS...*"
"... IN SOUTH-EAST AFRICA, *DELAGOA BAY* HAD BECOME A CRUEL CONFLUENCE FOR THE *SLAVE TRADE,* LIKE A *WOUND* IN THE *COASTLINE* ITSELF...
"... HERE, THE *MOST AVARICIOUS* OF LEADERS WOULD SELL THEIR COUNTRYMEN INTO *CHAINS* FOR THE *GLINT* OF *COPPER...*"
"... *THEY WERE DARK DAYS.*"
"*OUR STORY,* HOWEVER, BEGINS ON THE *DUSTY SAVANNA* OF OUR *OWN LANDS...*"
... SO, THESE BECOME *MY* CATTLE... AND NOW I HAVE THE *MOST.*
THIS IS *UNFAIR!* SHAKA IS *ALWAYS WINNING...* HE *MUST* BE *CHEATING!*

SUNSET, IN THE ZULU TERRITORIES...

AH, FORGET IT, SIGUJANA! SHAKA'S ALWAYS A MOVE AHEAD!

BUT DON'T WORRY, ALL HE'LL EVER BE GOOD AT IS PLAYING GAMES IN THE DUST!

HEY, BOYS....

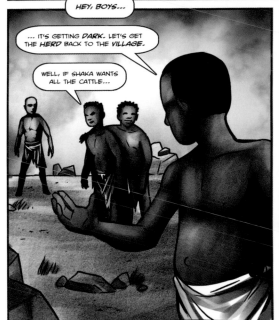

... IT'S GETTING DARK. LET'S GET THE HERD BACK TO THE VILLAGE.

WELL, IF SHAKA WANTS ALL THE CATTLE...

... THEN HE CAN BRING THEM HOME. COME ON, BROTHERS, WE'LL GO ON AHEAD.

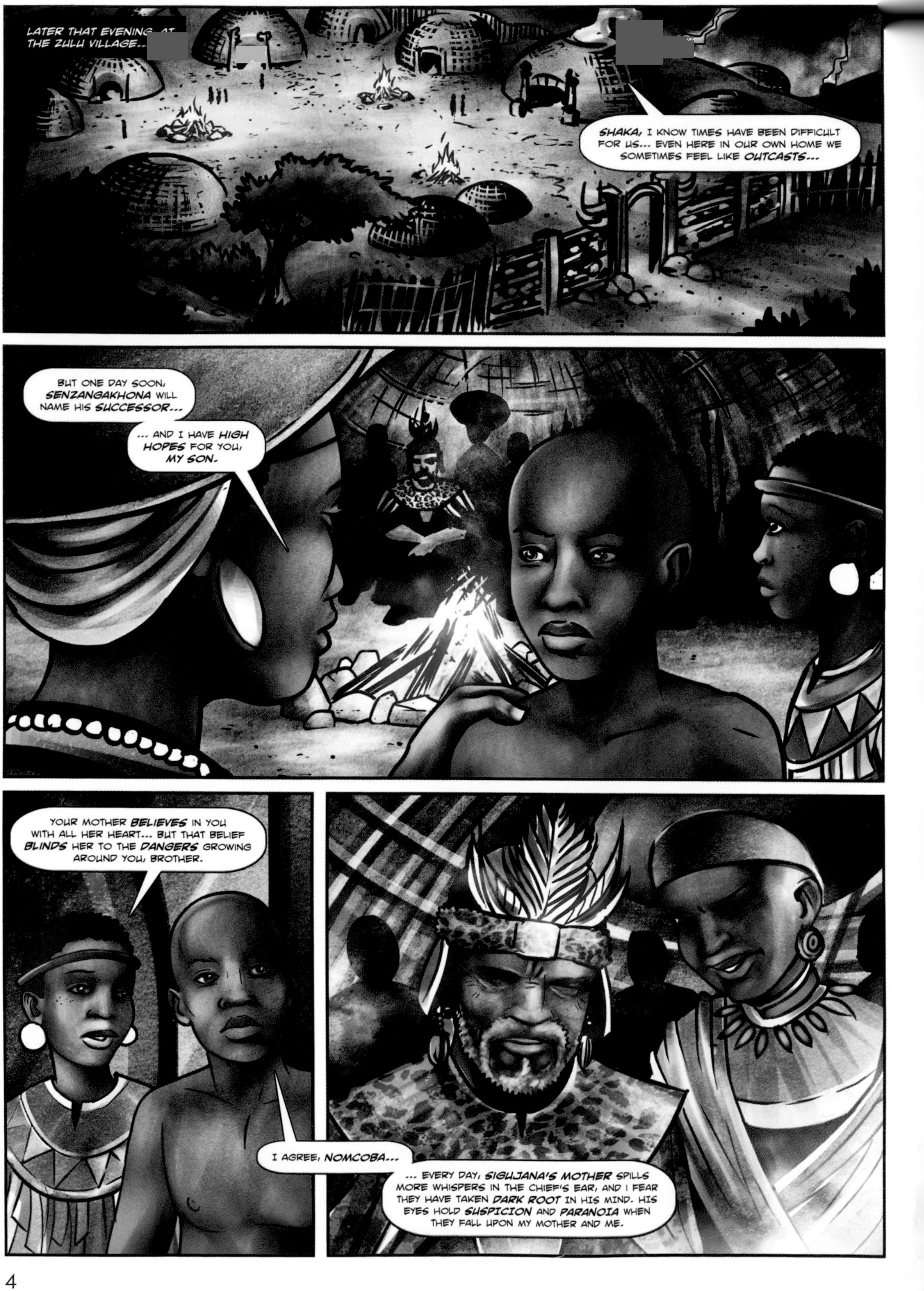
LATER THAT EVENING AT THE ZULU VILLAGE...
SHAKA, I KNOW TIMES HAVE BEEN DIFFICULT FOR US... EVEN HERE IN OUR OWN HOME WE SOMETIMES FEEL LIKE OUTCASTS...
BUT ONE DAY SOON, SENZANGAKHONA WILL NAME HIS SUCCESSOR...
... AND I HAVE HIGH HOPES FOR YOU, MY SON.
YOUR MOTHER BELIEVES IN YOU WITH ALL HER HEART... BUT THAT BELIEF BLINDS HER TO THE DANGERS GROWING AROUND YOU, BROTHER.
I AGREE, NOMCOBA...
... EVERY DAY, SIGUJANA'S MOTHER SPILLS MORE WHISPERS IN THE CHIEF'S EAR, AND I FEAR THEY HAVE TAKEN DARK ROOT IN HIS MIND. HIS EYES HOLD SUSPICION AND PARANOIA WHEN THEY FALL UPON MY MOTHER AND ME.

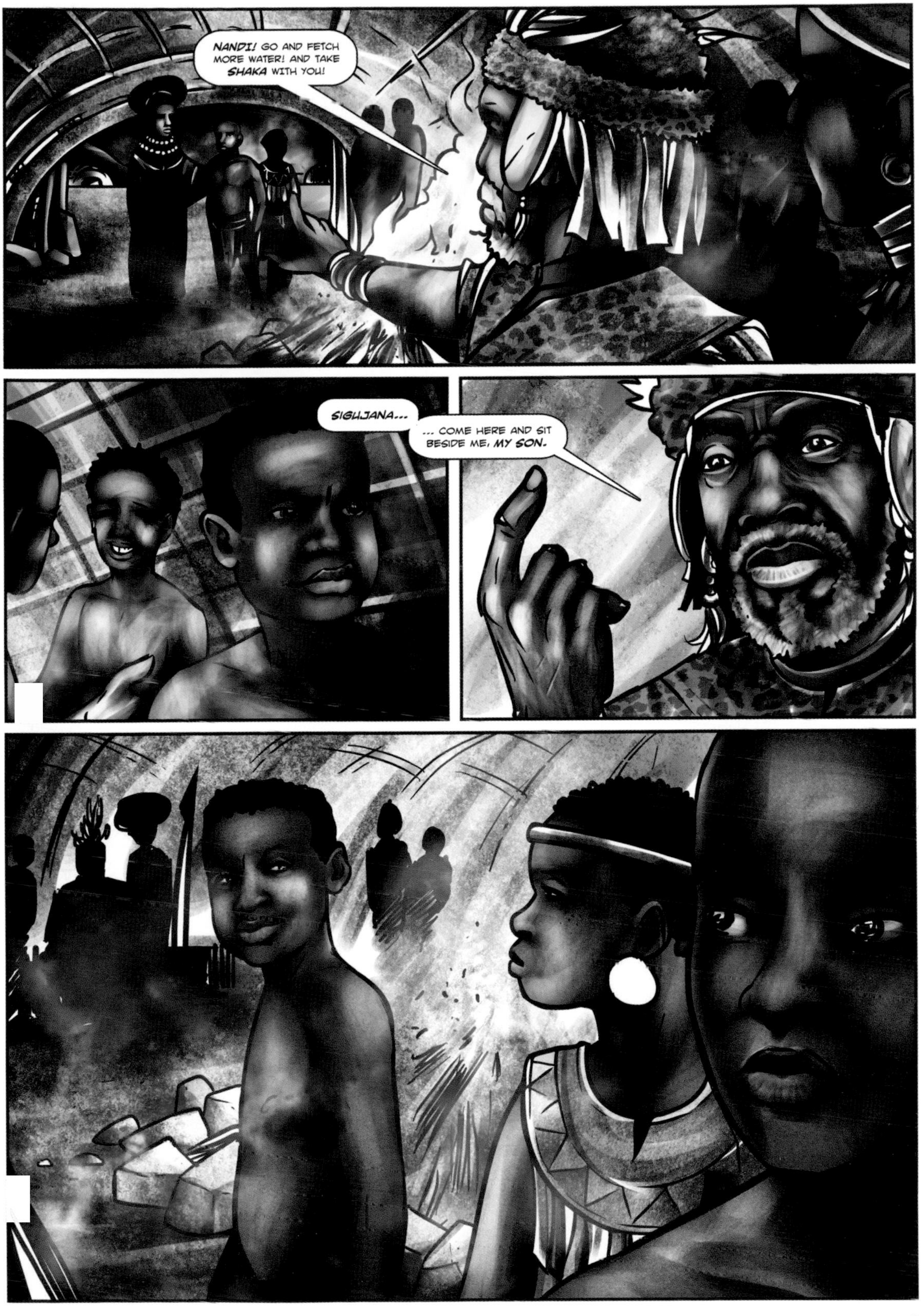
NANDI! GO AND FETCH MORE WATER! AND TAKE SHAKA WITH YOU!
SIGUJANA...
... COME HERE AND SIT BESIDE ME, MY SON.

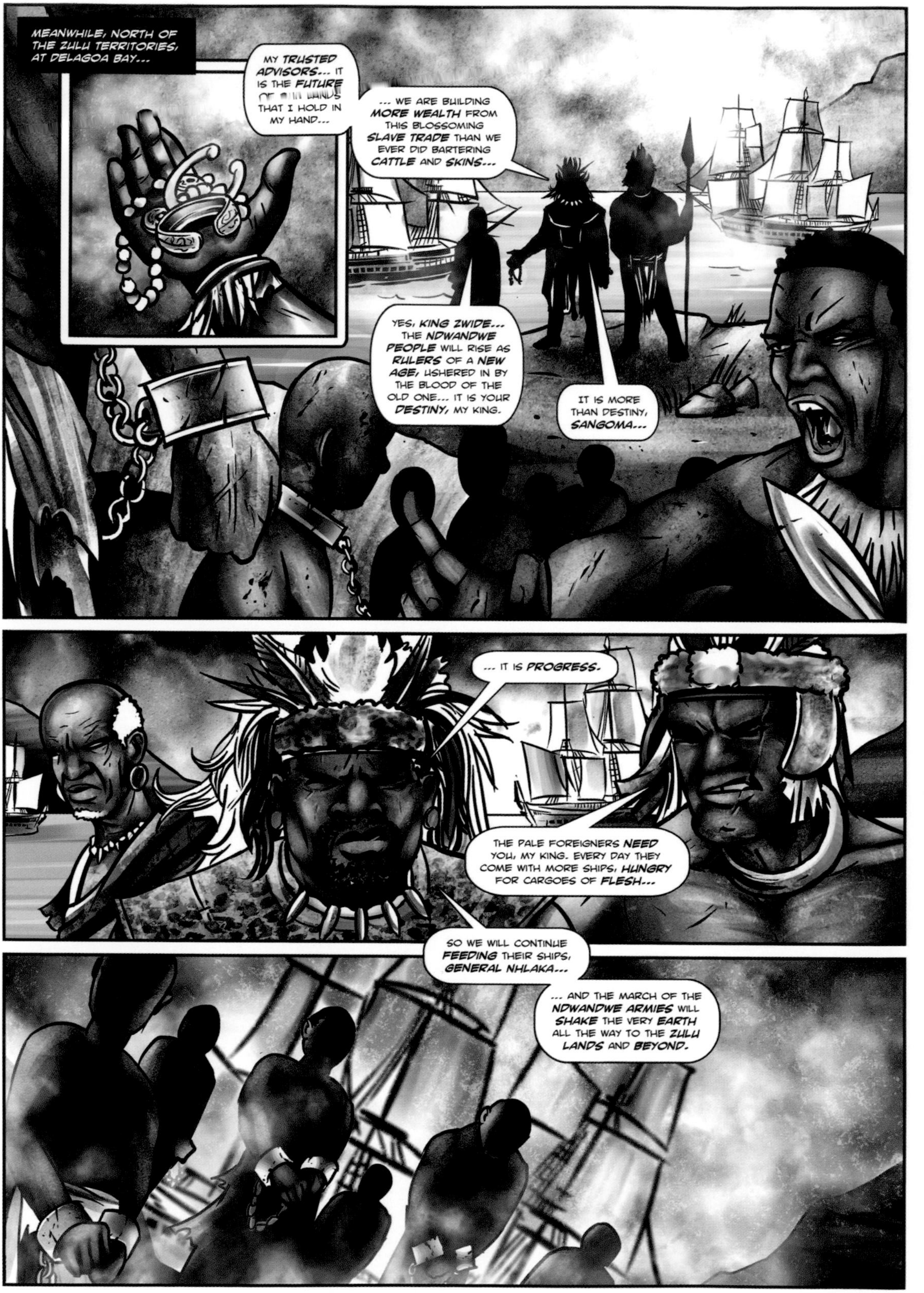
MEANWHILE, NORTH OF THE ZULU TERRITORIES, AT DELAGOA BAY...
MY TRUSTED ADVISORS... IT IS THE FUTURE THAT I HOLD IN MY HAND...
... WE ARE BUILDING MORE WEALTH FROM THIS BLOSSOMING SLAVE TRADE THAN WE EVER DID BARTERING CATTLE AND SKINS...
YES, KING ZWIDE... THE NDWANDWE PEOPLE WILL RISE AS RULERS OF A NEW AGE, USHERED IN BY THE BLOOD OF THE OLD ONE... IT IS YOUR DESTINY, MY KING.
IT IS MORE THAN DESTINY, SANGOMA...
... IT IS PROGRESS.
THE PALE FOREIGNERS NEED YOU, MY KING. EVERY DAY THEY COME WITH MORE SHIPS, HUNGRY FOR CARGOES OF FLESH...
SO WE WILL CONTINUE FEEDING THEIR SHIPS, GENERAL NHLAKA...
... AND THE MARCH OF THE NDWANDWE ARMIES WILL SHAKE THE VERY EARTH ALL THE WAY TO THE ZULU LANDS AND BEYOND.

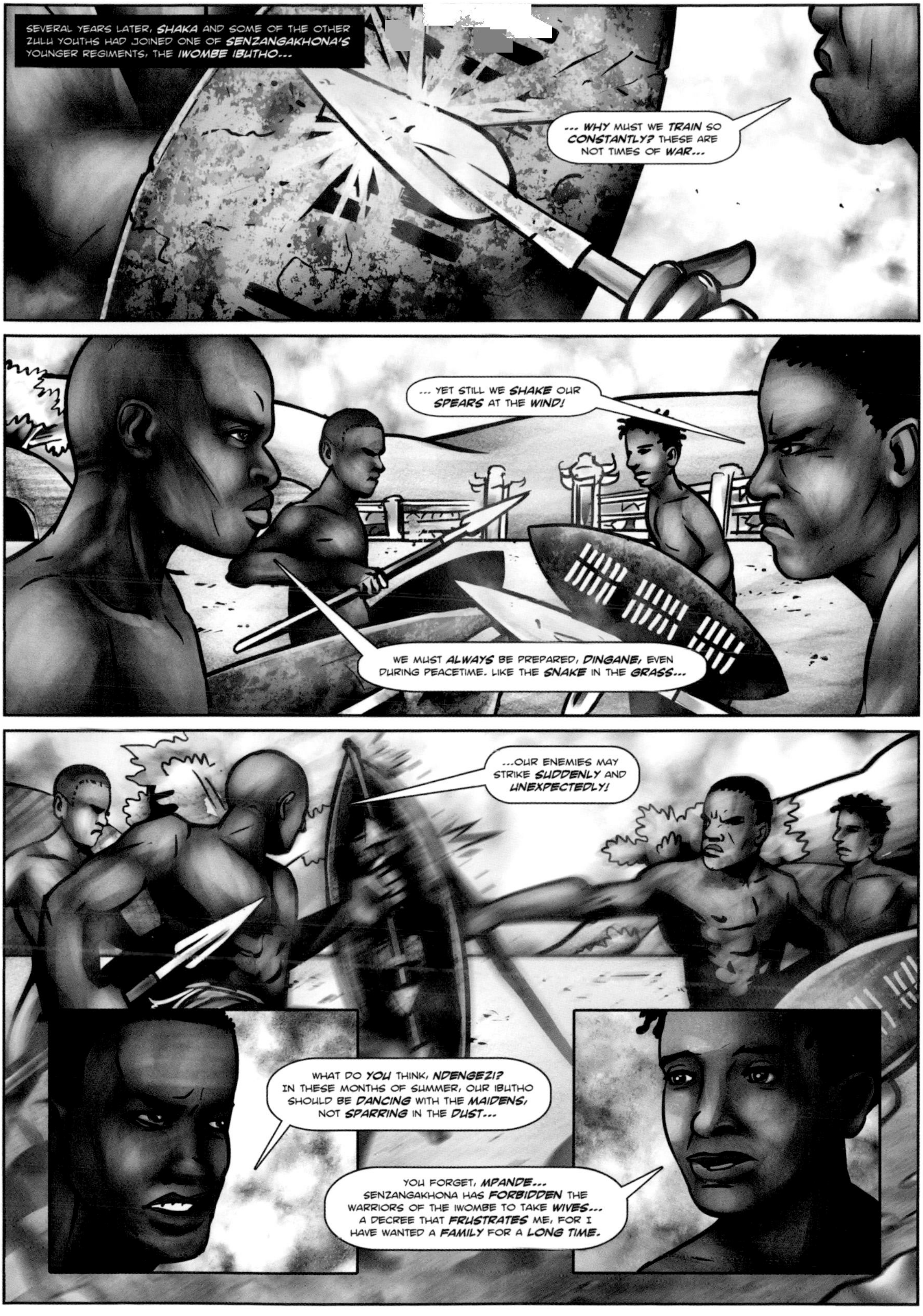
SEVERAL YEARS LATER, SHAKA AND SOME OF THE OTHER ZULU YOUTHS HAD JOINED ONE OF SENZANGAKHONA'S YOUNGER REGIMENTS, THE IWOMBE IBUTHO...
... WHY MUST WE TRAIN SO CONSTANTLY? THESE ARE NOT TIMES OF WAR...
... YET STILL WE SHAKE OUR SPEARS AT THE WIND!
WE MUST ALWAYS BE PREPARED, DINGANE, EVEN DURING PEACETIME. LIKE THE SNAKE IN THE GRASS...
...OUR ENEMIES MAY STRIKE SUDDENLY AND UNEXPECTEDLY!
WHAT DO YOU THINK, NDENGEZI? IN THESE MONTHS OF SUMMER, OUR IBUTHO SHOULD BE DANCING WITH THE MAIDENS, NOT SPARRING IN THE DUST...
YOU FORGET, MPANDE... SENZANGAKHONA HAS FORBIDDEN THE WARRIORS OF THE IWOMBE TO TAKE WIVES... A DECREE THAT FRUSTRATES ME, FOR I HAVE WANTED A FAMILY FOR A LONG TIME.

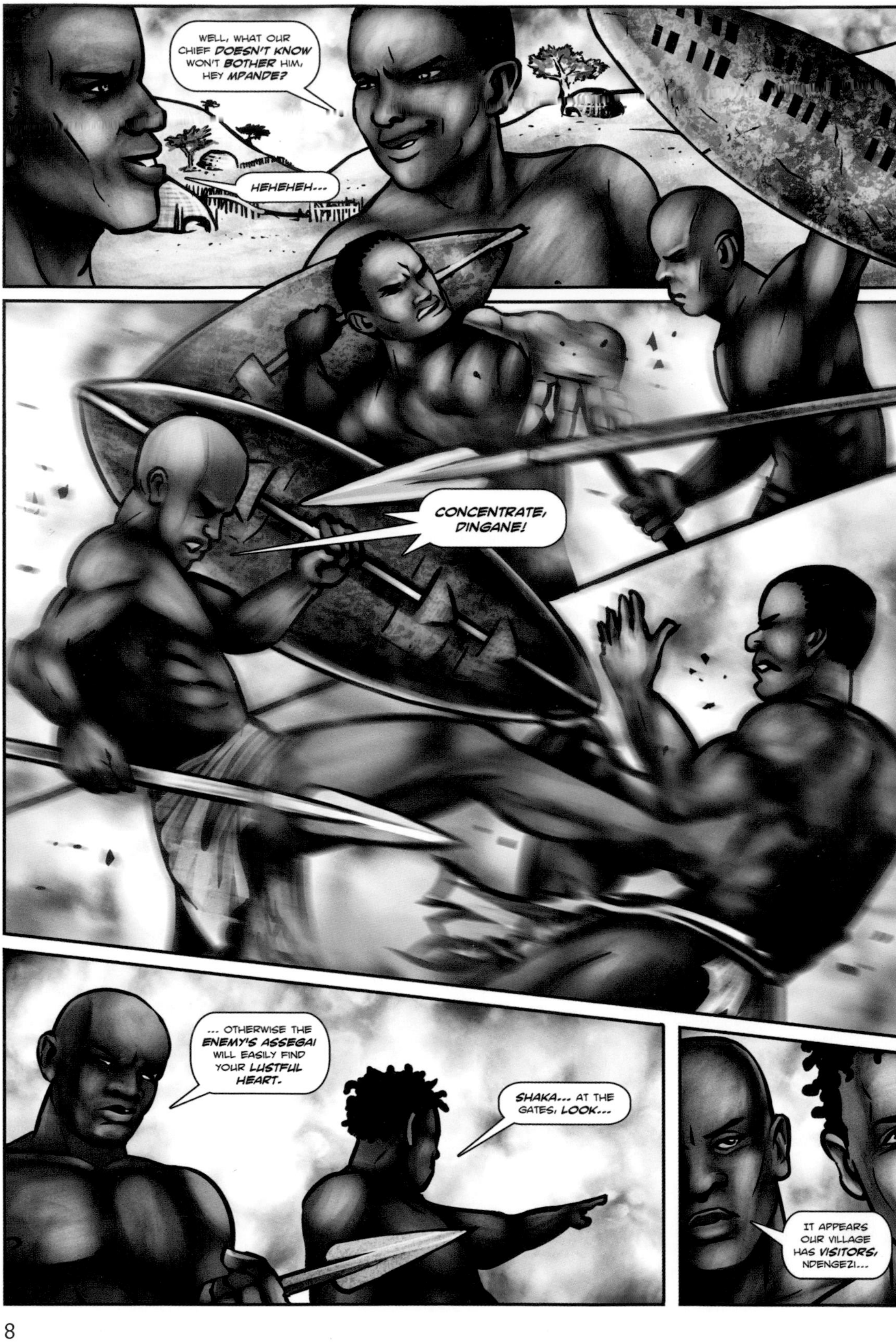
WELL, WHAT OUR CHIEF DOESN'T KNOW WON'T BOTHER HIM, HEY MPANDE?
HEHEHEH...
CONCENTRATE, DINGANE!
... OTHERWISE THE ENEMY'S ASSEGAI WILL EASILY FIND YOUR LUSTFUL HEART.
SHAKA... AT THE GATES, LOOK...
IT APPEARS OUR VILLAGE HAS VISITORS, NDENGEZI...

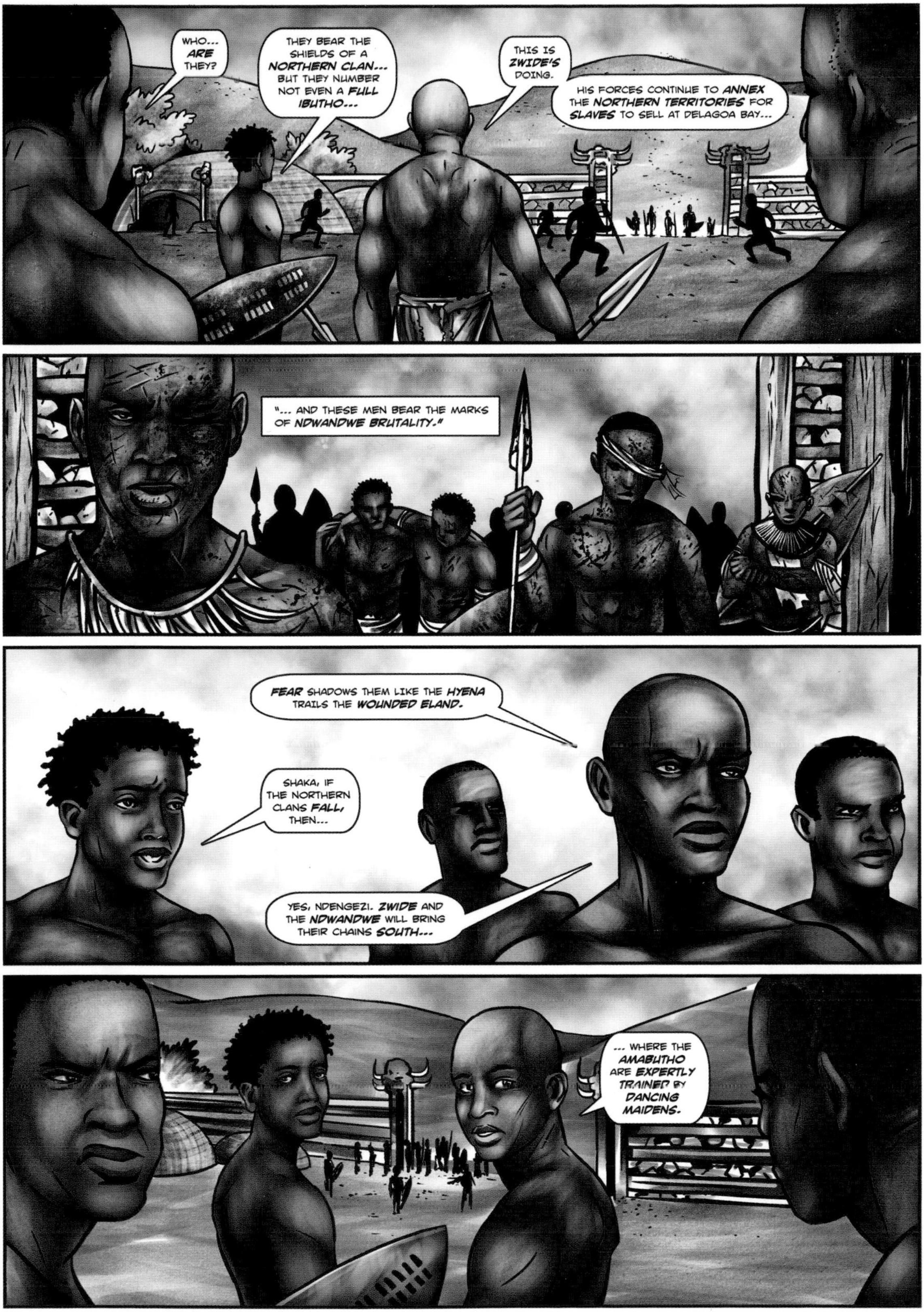
WHO... ARE THEY?
THEY BEAR THE SHIELDS OF A NORTHERN CLAN... BUT THEY NUMBER NOT EVEN A FULL IBUTHO...
THIS IS ZWIDE'S DOING.
HIS FORCES CONTINUE TO ANNEX THE NORTHERN TERRITORIES FOR SLAVES TO SELL AT DELAGOA BAY...
"... AND THESE MEN BEAR THE MARKS OF NDWANDWE BRUTALITY."
FEAR SHADOWS THEM LIKE THE HYENA TRAILS THE WOUNDED ELAND.
SHAKA, IF THE NORTHERN CLANS FALL, THEN...
YES, NDENGEZI. ZWIDE AND THE NDWANDWE WILL BRING THEIR CHAINS SOUTH...
... WHERE THE AMABUTHO ARE EXPERTLY TRAINED BY DANCING MAIDENS.

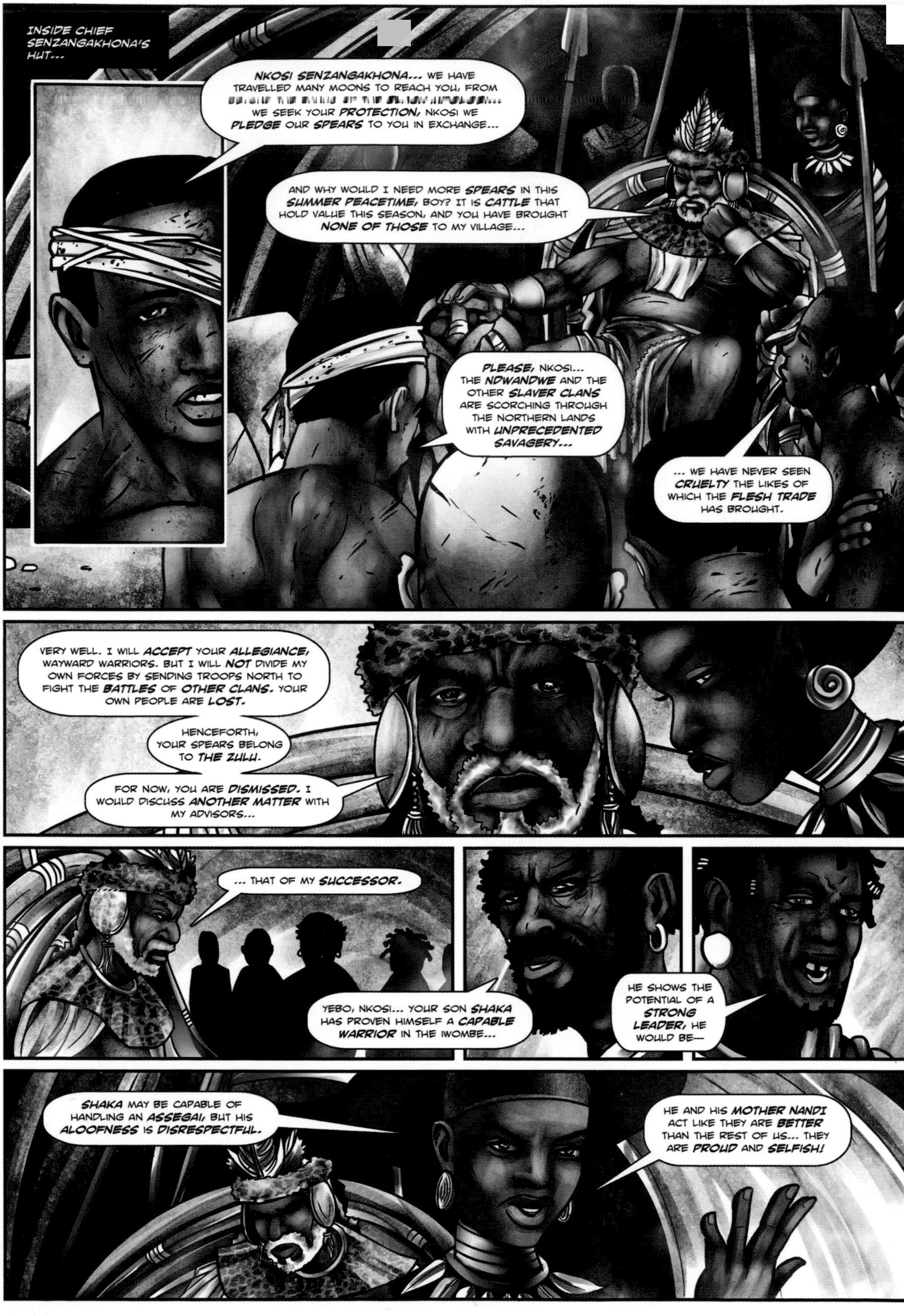
INSIDE CHIEF SENZANGAKHONA'S HUT...
NKOSI SENZANGAKHONA... WE HAVE TRAVELLED MANY MOONS TO REACH YOU, FROM
WE SEEK YOUR PROTECTION, NKOSI WE PLEDGE OUR SPEARS TO YOU IN EXCHANGE...
AND WHY WOULD I NEED MORE SPEARS IN THIS SUMMER PEACETIME, BOY? IT IS CATTLE THAT HOLD VALUE THIS SEASON, AND YOU HAVE BROUGHT NONE OF THOSE TO MY VILLAGE...
PLEASE, NKOSI... THE NDWANDWE AND THE OTHER SLAVER CLANS ARE SCORCHING THROUGH THE NORTHERN LANDS WITH UNPRECEDENTED SAVAGERY...
... WE HAVE NEVER SEEN CRUELTY THE LIKES OF WHICH THE FLESH TRADE HAS BROUGHT.
VERY WELL. I WILL ACCEPT YOUR ALLEGIANCE, WAYWARD WARRIORS. BUT I WILL NOT DIVIDE MY OWN FORCES BY SENDING TROOPS NORTH TO FIGHT THE BATTLES OF OTHER CLANS. YOUR OWN PEOPLE ARE LOST.
HENCEFORTH, YOUR SPEARS BELONG TO THE ZULU.
FOR NOW, YOU ARE DISMISSED. I WOULD DISCUSS ANOTHER MATTER WITH MY ADVISORS...
... THAT OF MY SUCCESSOR.
YEBO, NKOSI... YOUR SON SHAKA HAS PROVEN HIMSELF A CAPABLE WARRIOR IN THE IWOMBE...
HE SHOWS THE POTENTIAL OF A STRONG LEADER, HE WOULD BE—
SHAKA MAY BE CAPABLE OF HANDLING AN ASSEGAI, BUT HIS ALOOFNESS IS DISRESPECTFUL.
HE AND HIS MOTHER NANDI ACT LIKE THEY ARE BETTER THAN THE REST OF US... THEY ARE PROUD AND SELFISH!

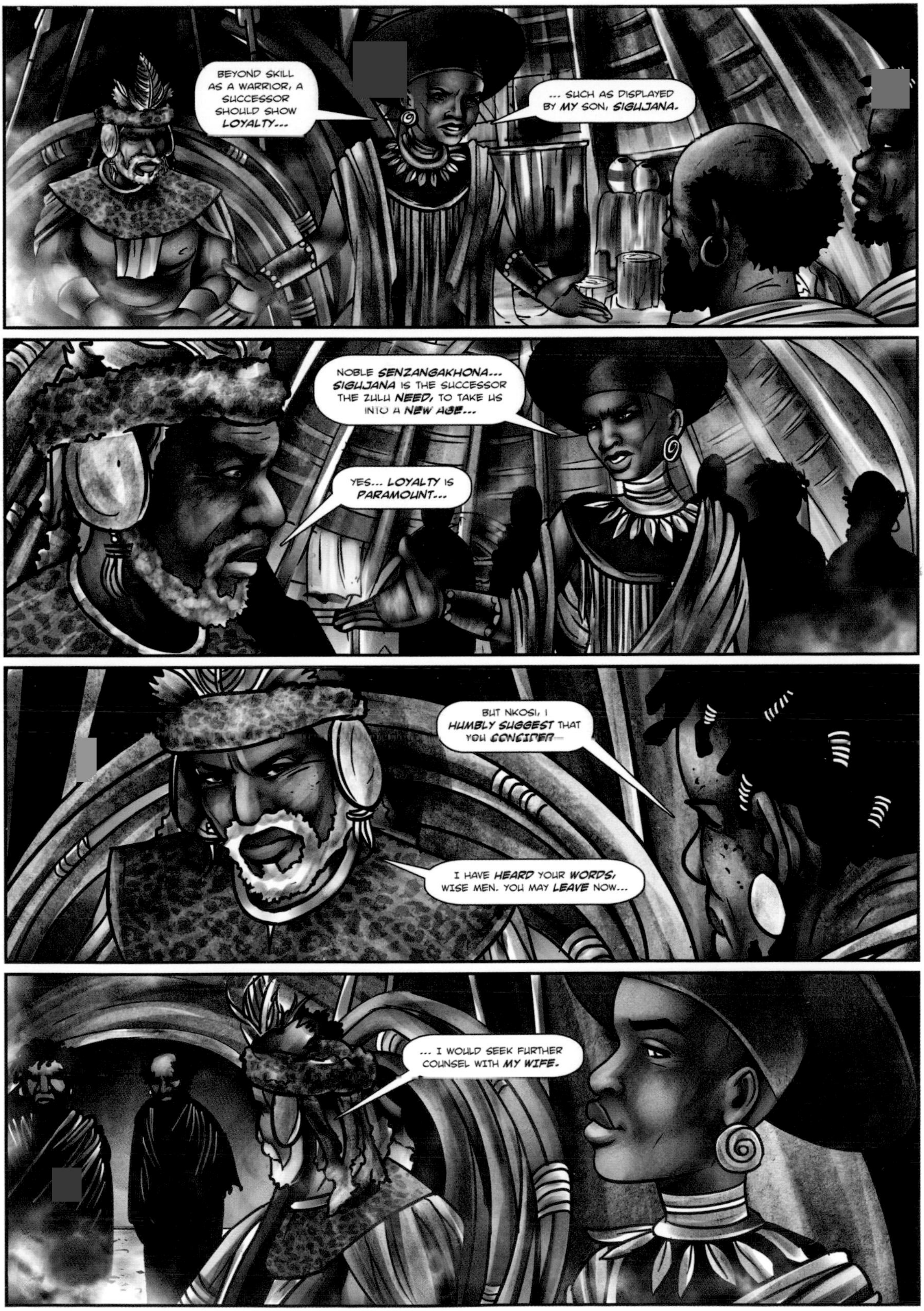
BEYOND SKILL AS A WARRIOR, A SUCCESSOR SHOULD SHOW LOYALTY...
... SUCH AS DISPLAYED BY MY SON, SIGUJANA.
NOBLE SENZANGAKHONA... SIGUJANA IS THE SUCCESSOR THE ZULU NEED, TO TAKE US INTO A NEW AGE...
YES... LOYALTY IS PARAMOUNT...
BUT NKOSI, I HUMBLY SUGGEST THAT YOU CONCIDER—
I HAVE HEARD YOUR WORDS, WISE MEN. YOU MAY LEAVE NOW...
... I WOULD SEEK FURTHER COUNSEL WITH MY WIFE.

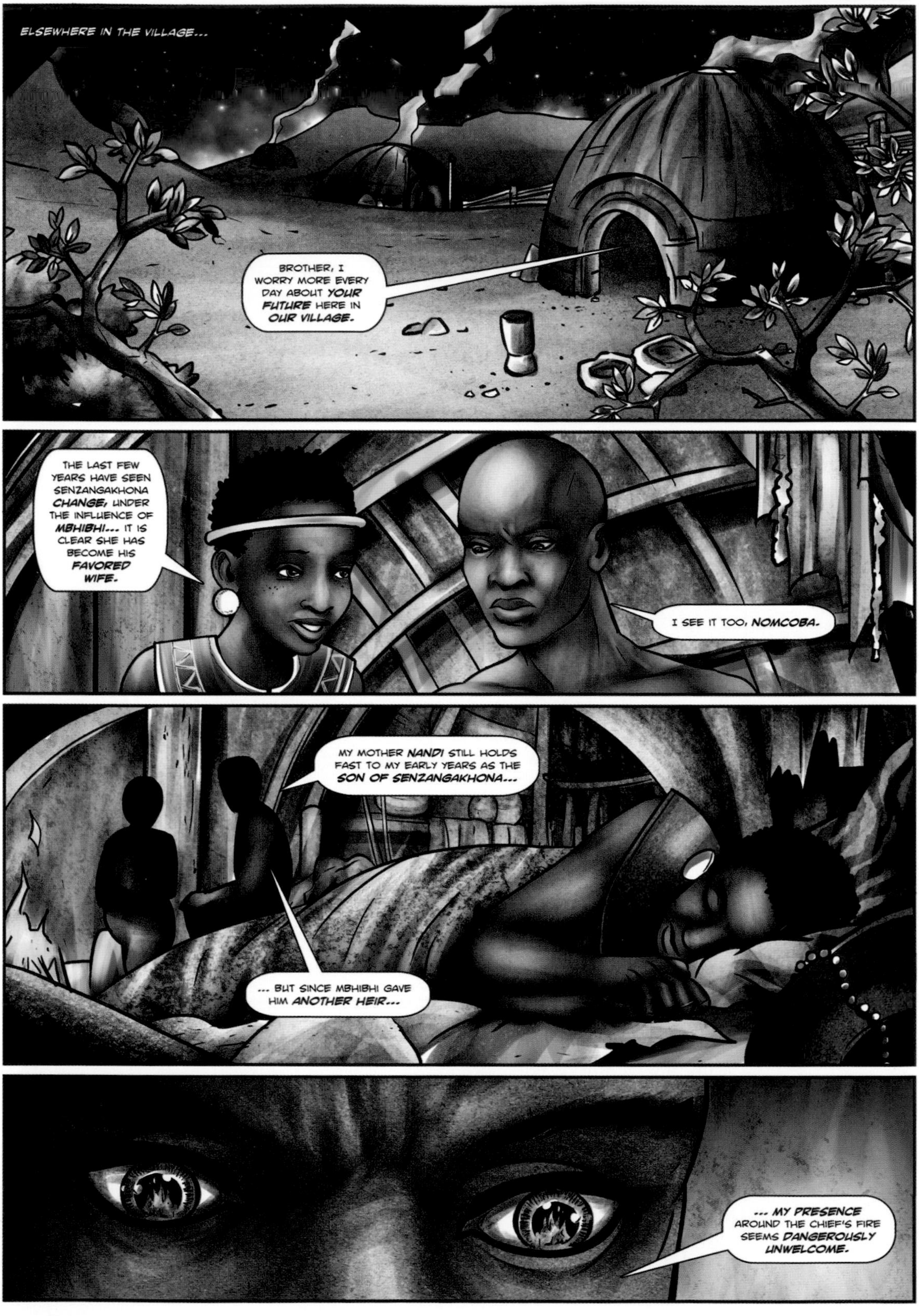
ELSEWHERE IN THE VILLAGE...
BROTHER, I WORRY MORE EVERY DAY ABOUT YOUR FUTURE HERE IN OUR VILLAGE.
THE LAST FEW YEARS HAVE SEEN SENZANGAKHONA CHANGE, UNDER THE INFLUENCE OF MBHIBHI... IT IS CLEAR SHE HAS BECOME HIS FAVORED WIFE.
I SEE IT TOO, NOMCOBA.
MY MOTHER NANDI STILL HOLDS FAST TO MY EARLY YEARS AS THE SON OF SENZANGAKHONA...
... BUT SINCE MBHIBHI GAVE HIM ANOTHER HEIR...
... MY PRESENCE AROUND THE CHIEF'S FIRE SEEMS DANGEROUSLY UNWELCOME.

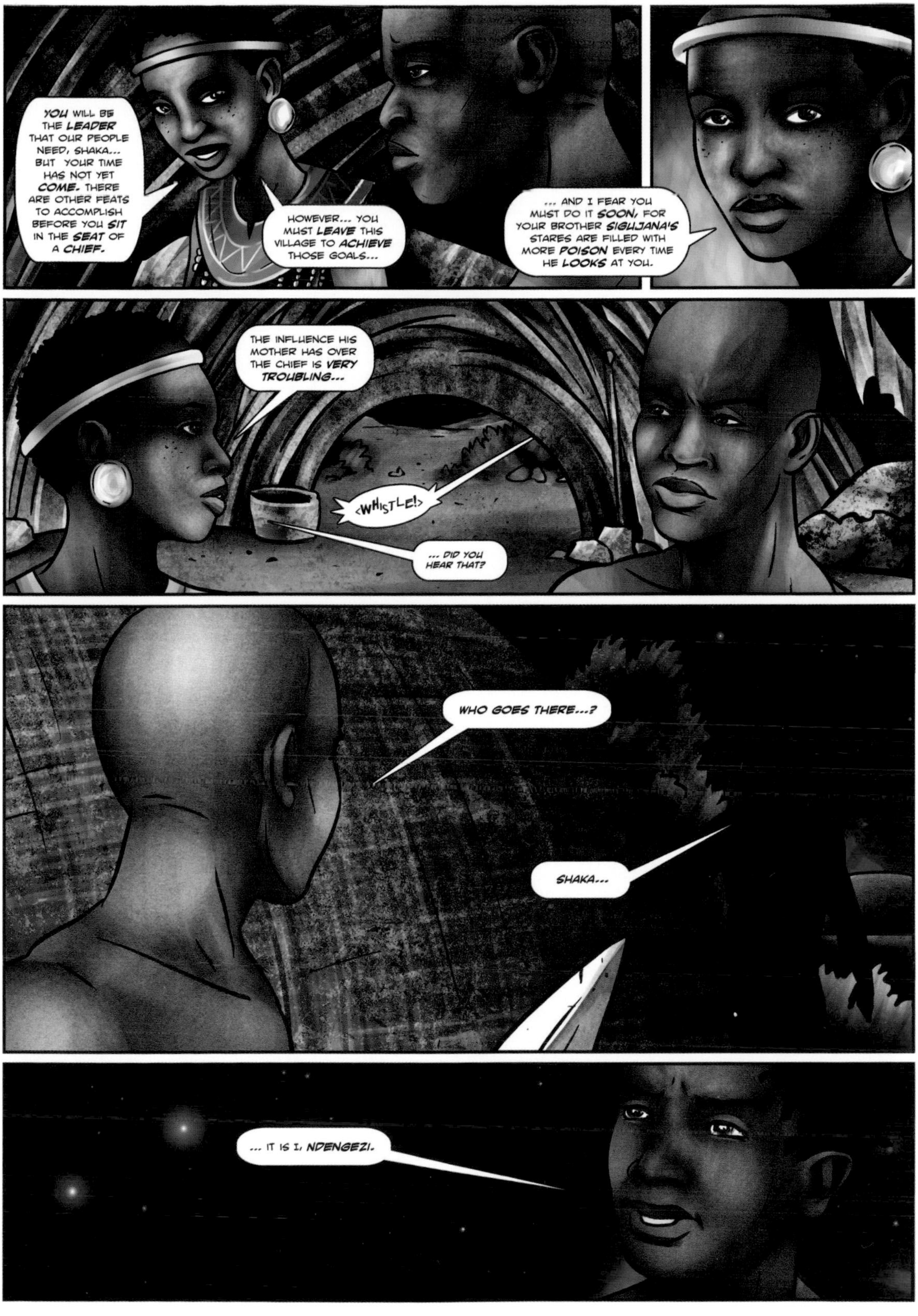
YOU WILL BE THE LEADER THAT OUR PEOPLE NEED, SHAKA... BUT YOUR TIME HAS NOT YET COME. THERE ARE OTHER FEATS TO ACCOMPLISH BEFORE YOU SIT IN THE SEAT OF A CHIEF.
HOWEVER... YOU MUST LEAVE THIS VILLAGE TO ACHIEVE THOSE GOALS...
... AND I FEAR YOU MUST DO IT SOON, FOR YOUR BROTHER SIGUJANA'S STARES ARE FILLED WITH MORE POISON EVERY TIME HE LOOKS AT YOU.
THE INFLUENCE HIS MOTHER HAS OVER THE CHIEF IS VERY TROUBLING...
<WHISTLE!>
... DID YOU HEAR THAT?
WHO GOES THERE...?
SHAKA...
... IT IS I, NDENGEZI.

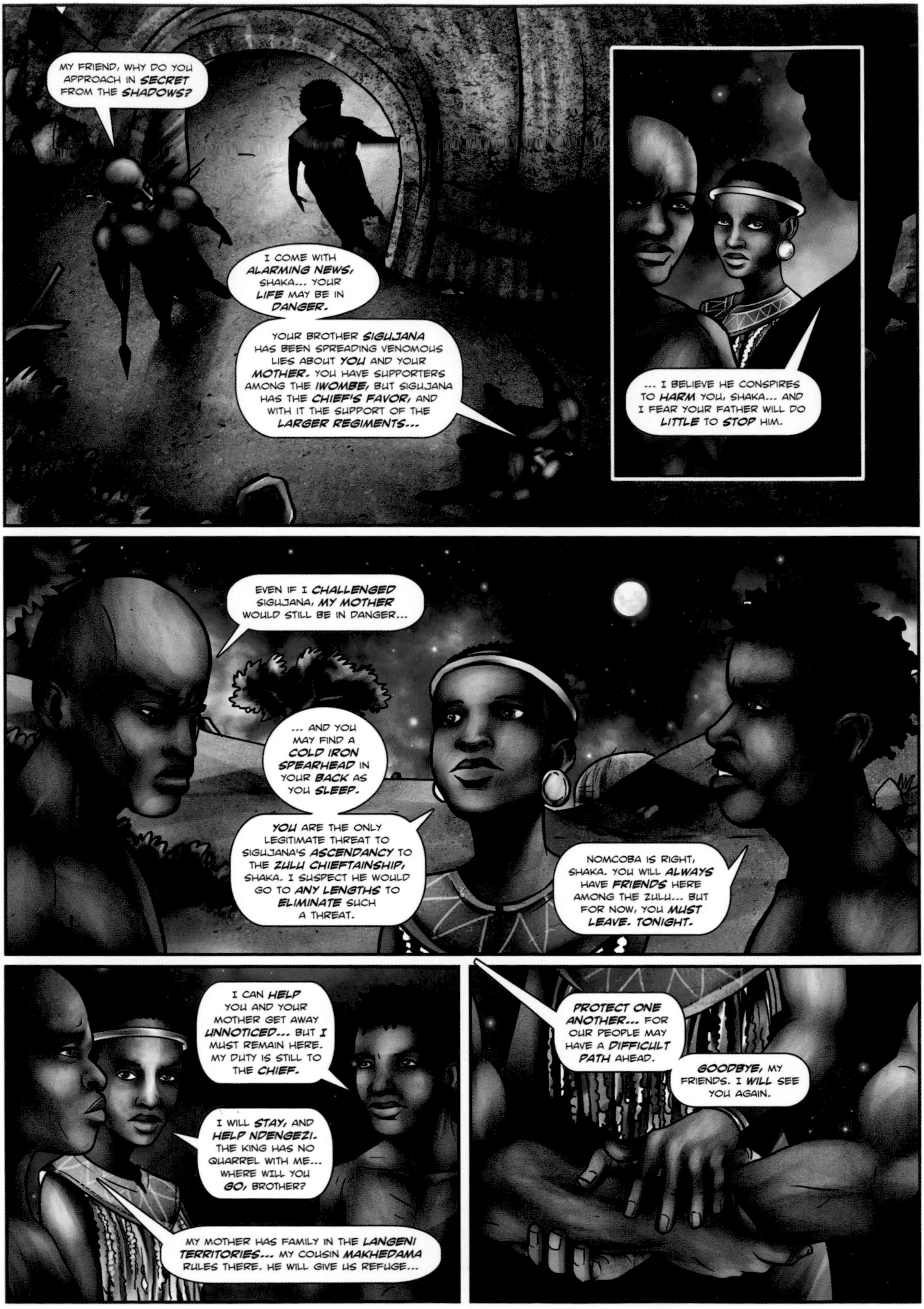

MY FRIEND, WHY DO YOU APPROACH IN SECRET FROM THE SHADOWS?
I COME WITH ALARMING NEWS, SHAKA... YOUR LIFE MAY BE IN DANGER.
YOUR BROTHER SIGUJANA HAS BEEN SPREADING VENOMOUS LIES ABOUT YOU AND YOUR MOTHER. YOU HAVE SUPPORTERS AMONG THE IWOMBE, BUT SIGUJANA HAS THE CHIEF'S FAVOR, AND WITH IT THE SUPPORT OF THE LARGER REGIMENTS...
... I BELIEVE HE CONSPIRES TO HARM YOU, SHAKA... AND I FEAR YOUR FATHER WILL DO LITTLE TO STOP HIM.
EVEN IF I CHALLENGED SIGUJANA, MY MOTHER WOULD STILL BE IN DANGER...
... AND YOU MAY FIND A COLD IRON SPEARHEAD IN YOUR BACK AS YOU SLEEP.
YOU ARE THE ONLY LEGITIMATE THREAT TO SIGUJANA'S ASCENDANCY TO THE ZULU CHIEFTAINSHIP, SHAKA. I SUSPECT HE WOULD GO TO ANY LENGTHS TO ELIMINATE SUCH A THREAT.
NOMCOBA IS RIGHT, SHAKA. YOU WILL ALWAYS HAVE FRIENDS HERE AMONG THE ZULU... BUT FOR NOW, YOU MUST LEAVE. TONIGHT.
I CAN HELP YOU AND YOUR MOTHER GET AWAY UNNOTICED... BUT I MUST REMAIN HERE. MY DUTY IS STILL TO THE CHIEF.
I WILL STAY, AND HELP NDENGEZI. THE KING HAS NO QUARREL WITH ME... WHERE WILL YOU GO, BROTHER?
MY MOTHER HAS FAMILY IN THE LANGENI TERRITORIES... MY COUSIN MAKHEDAMA RULES THERE. HE WILL GIVE US REFUGE...
PROTECT ONE ANOTHER... FOR OUR PEOPLE MAY HAVE A DIFFICULT PATH AHEAD.
GOODBYE, MY FRIENDS. I WILL SEE YOU AGAIN.

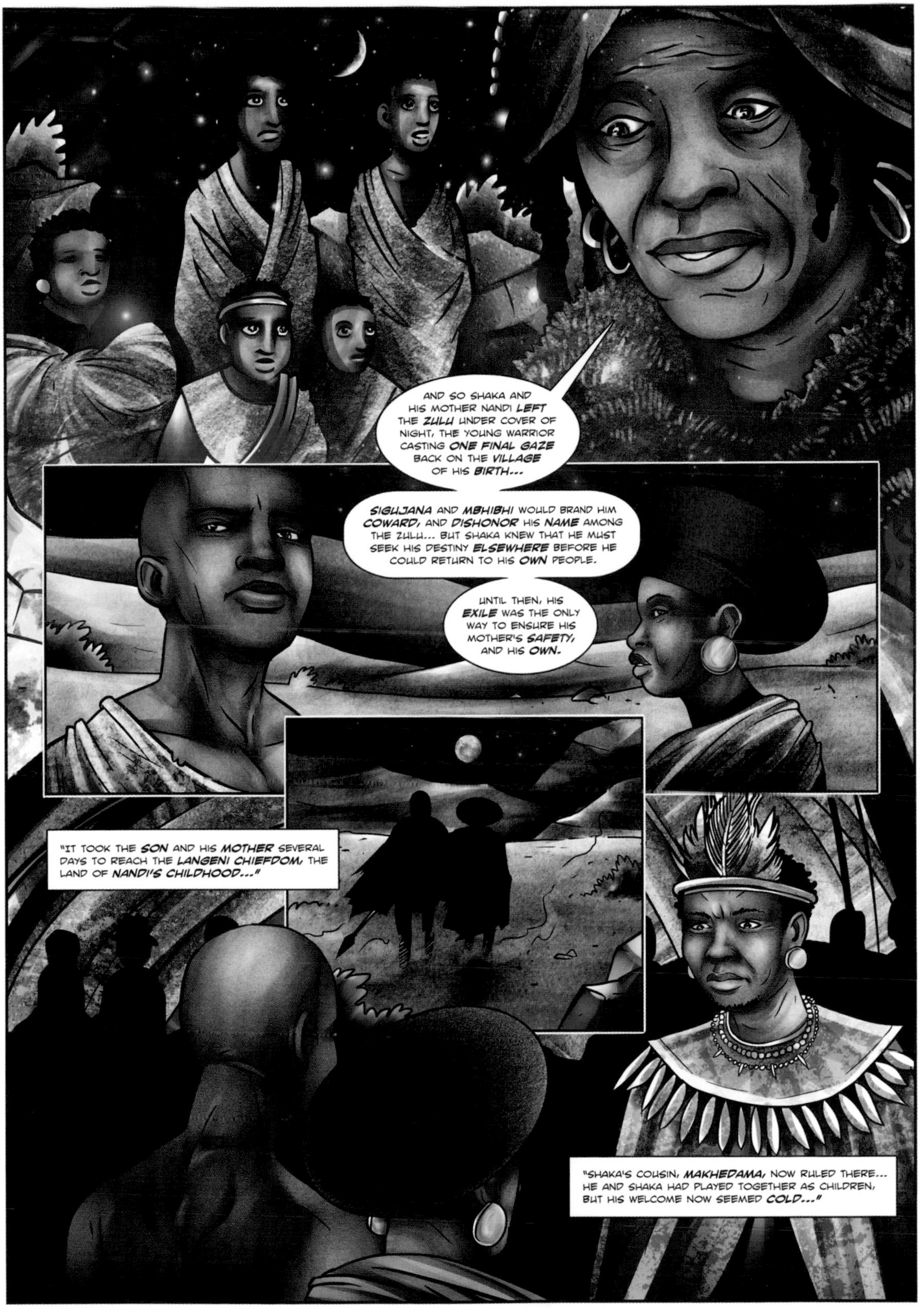

AND SO SHAKA AND HIS MOTHER NANDI LEFT THE ZULU UNDER COVER OF NIGHT, THE YOUNG WARRIOR CASTING ONE FINAL GAZE BACK ON THE VILLAGE OF HIS BIRTH...
SIGUJANA AND MBHIBHI WOULD BRAND HIM COWARD, AND DISHONOR HIS NAME AMONG THE ZULU... BUT SHAKA KNEW THAT HE MUST SEEK HIS DESTINY ELSEWHERE BEFORE HE COULD RETURN TO HIS OWN PEOPLE.
UNTIL THEN, HIS EXILE WAS THE ONLY WAY TO ENSURE HIS MOTHER'S SAFETY, AND HIS OWN.
"IT TOOK THE SON AND HIS MOTHER SEVERAL DAYS TO REACH THE LANGENI CHIEFDOM, THE LAND OF NANDI'S CHILDHOOD..."
"SHAKA'S COUSIN, MAKHEDAMA, NOW RULED THERE... HE AND SHAKA HAD PLAYED TOGETHER AS CHILDREN, BUT HIS WELCOME NOW SEEMED COLD..."

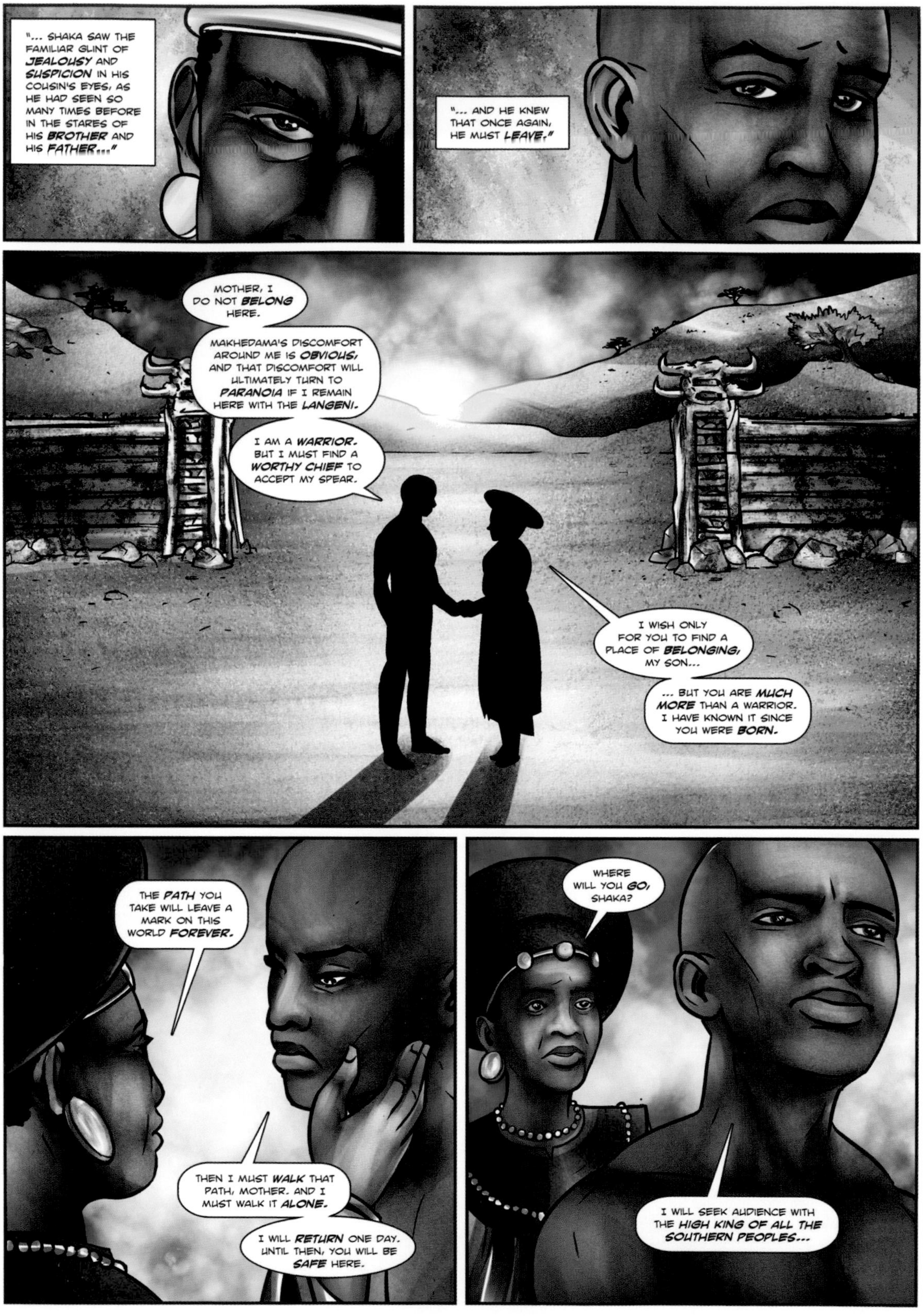
"... SHAKA SAW THE FAMILIAR GLINT OF JEALOUSY AND SUSPICION IN HIS COUSIN'S EYES, AS HE HAD SEEN SO MANY TIMES BEFORE IN THE STARES OF HIS BROTHER AND HIS FATHER..."
"... AND HE KNEW THAT ONCE AGAIN, HE MUST LEAVE."
MOTHER, I DO NOT BELONG HERE.
MAKHEDAMA'S DISCOMFORT AROUND ME IS OBVIOUS, AND THAT DISCOMFORT WILL ULTIMATELY TURN TO PARANOIA IF I REMAIN HERE WITH THE LANGENI.
I AM A WARRIOR. BUT I MUST FIND A WORTHY CHIEF TO ACCEPT MY SPEAR.
I WISH ONLY FOR YOU TO FIND A PLACE OF BELONGING, MY SON...
... BUT YOU ARE MUCH MORE THAN A WARRIOR. I HAVE KNOWN IT SINCE YOU WERE BORN.
THE PATH YOU TAKE WILL LEAVE A MARK ON THIS WORLD FOREVER.
THEN I MUST WALK THAT PATH, MOTHER. AND I MUST WALK IT ALONE.
I WILL RETURN ONE DAY. UNTIL THEN, YOU WILL BE SAFE HERE.
WHERE WILL YOU GO, SHAKA?
I WILL SEEK AUDIENCE WITH THE HIGH KING OF ALL THE SOUTHERN PEOPLES...

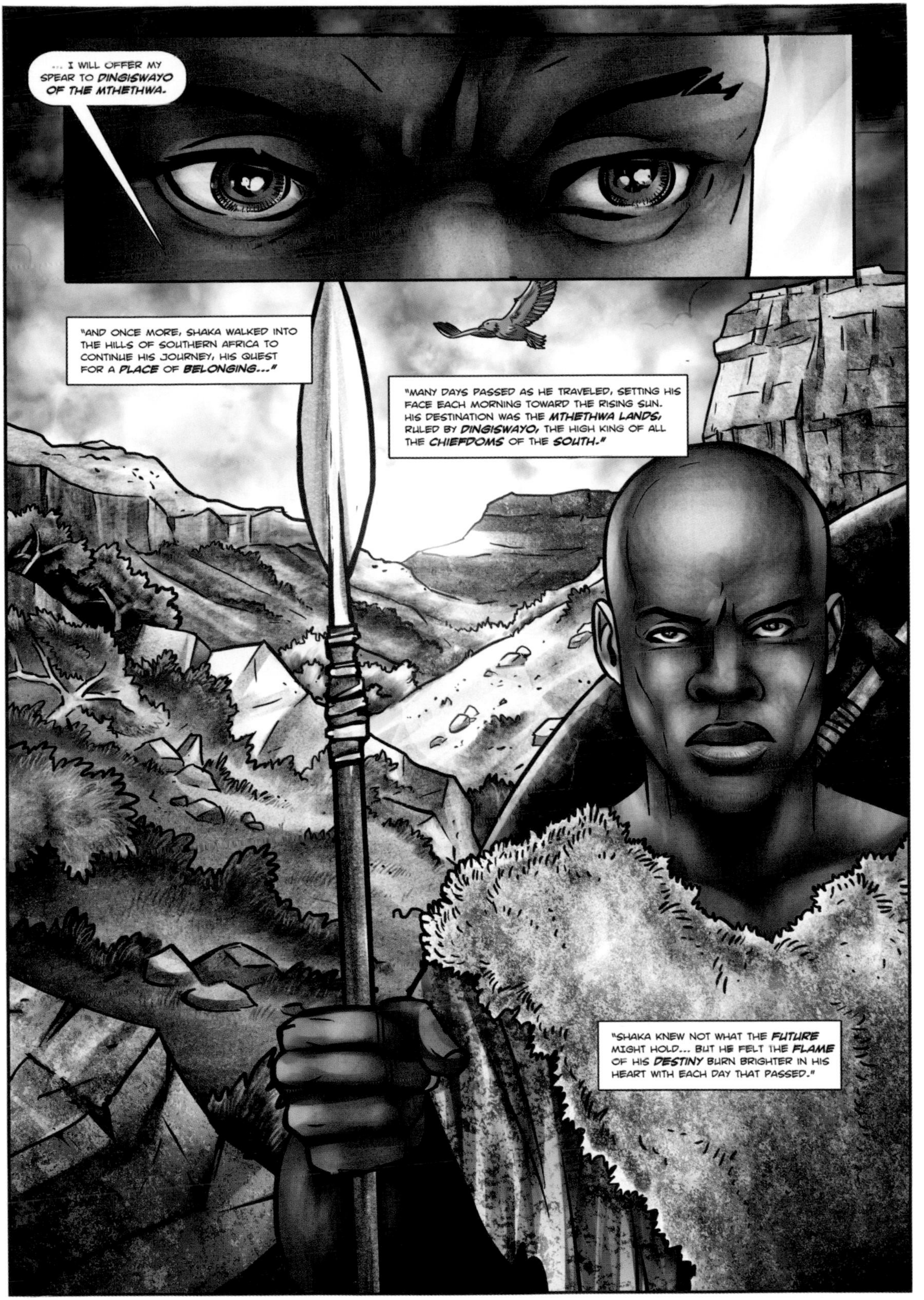
... I WILL OFFER MY SPEAR TO DINGISWAYO OF THE MTHETHWA.
"AND ONCE MORE, SHAKA WALKED INTO THE HILLS OF SOUTHERN AFRICA TO CONTINUE HIS JOURNEY, HIS QUEST FOR A PLACE OF BELONGING..."
"MANY DAYS PASSED AS HE TRAVELED, SETTING HIS FACE EACH MORNING TOWARD THE RISING SUN. HIS DESTINATION WAS THE MTHETHWA LANDS, RULED BY DINGISWAYO, THE HIGH KING OF ALL THE CHIEFDOMS OF THE SOUTH."
"SHAKA KNEW NOT WHAT THE FUTURE MIGHT HOLD... BUT HE FELT THE FLAME OF HIS DESTINY BURN BRIGHTER IN HIS HEART WITH EACH DAY THAT PASSED."

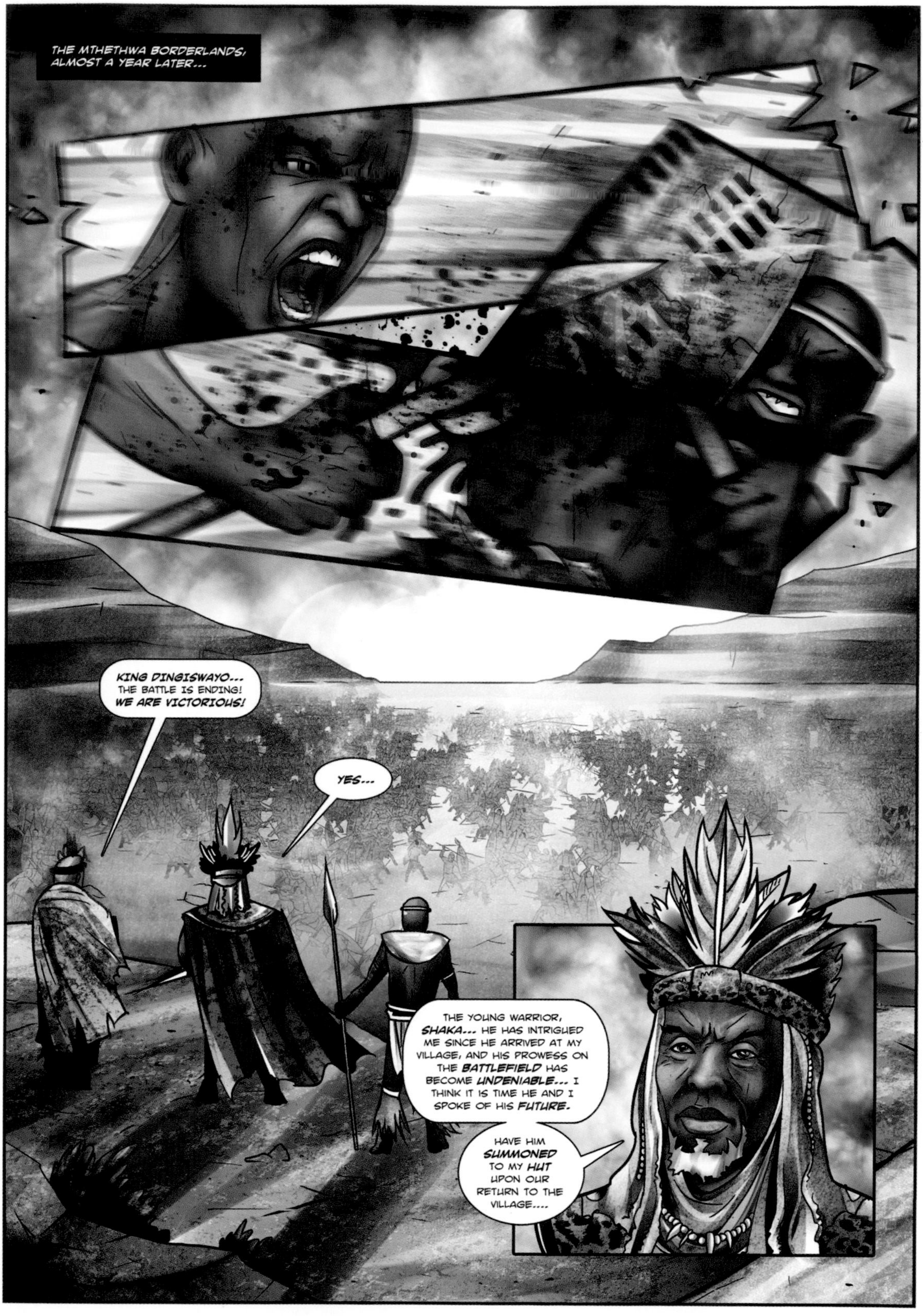
THE MTHETHWA BORDERLANDS, ALMOST A YEAR LATER...
KING DINGISWAYO... THE BATTLE IS ENDING! WE ARE VICTORIOUS!
YES...
THE YOUNG WARRIOR, SHAKA... HE HAS INTRIGUED ME SINCE HE ARRIVED AT MY VILLAGE, AND HIS PROWESS ON THE BATTLEFIELD HAS BECOME UNDENIABLE... I THINK IT IS TIME HE AND I SPOKE OF HIS FUTURE.
HAVE HIM SUMMONED TO MY HUT UPON OUR RETURN TO THE VILLAGE....

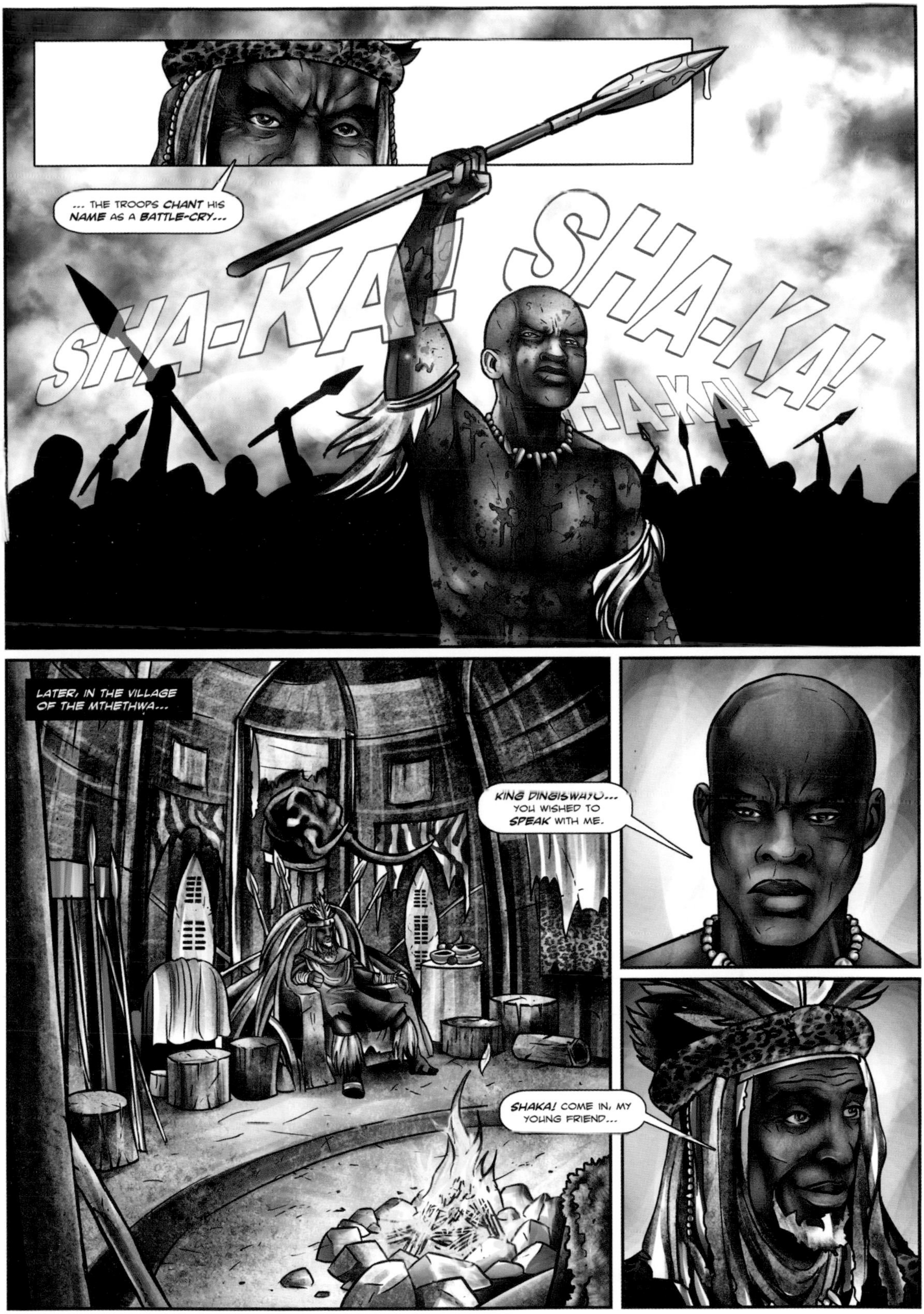
... THE TROOPS CHANT HIS NAME AS A BATTLE-CRY...
SHA-KA! SHA-KA!
SHA-KA!
LATER, IN THE VILLAGE OF THE MTHETHWA...
KING DINGISWAYO... YOU WISHED TO SPEAK WITH ME.
SHAKA! COME IN, MY YOUNG FRIEND...

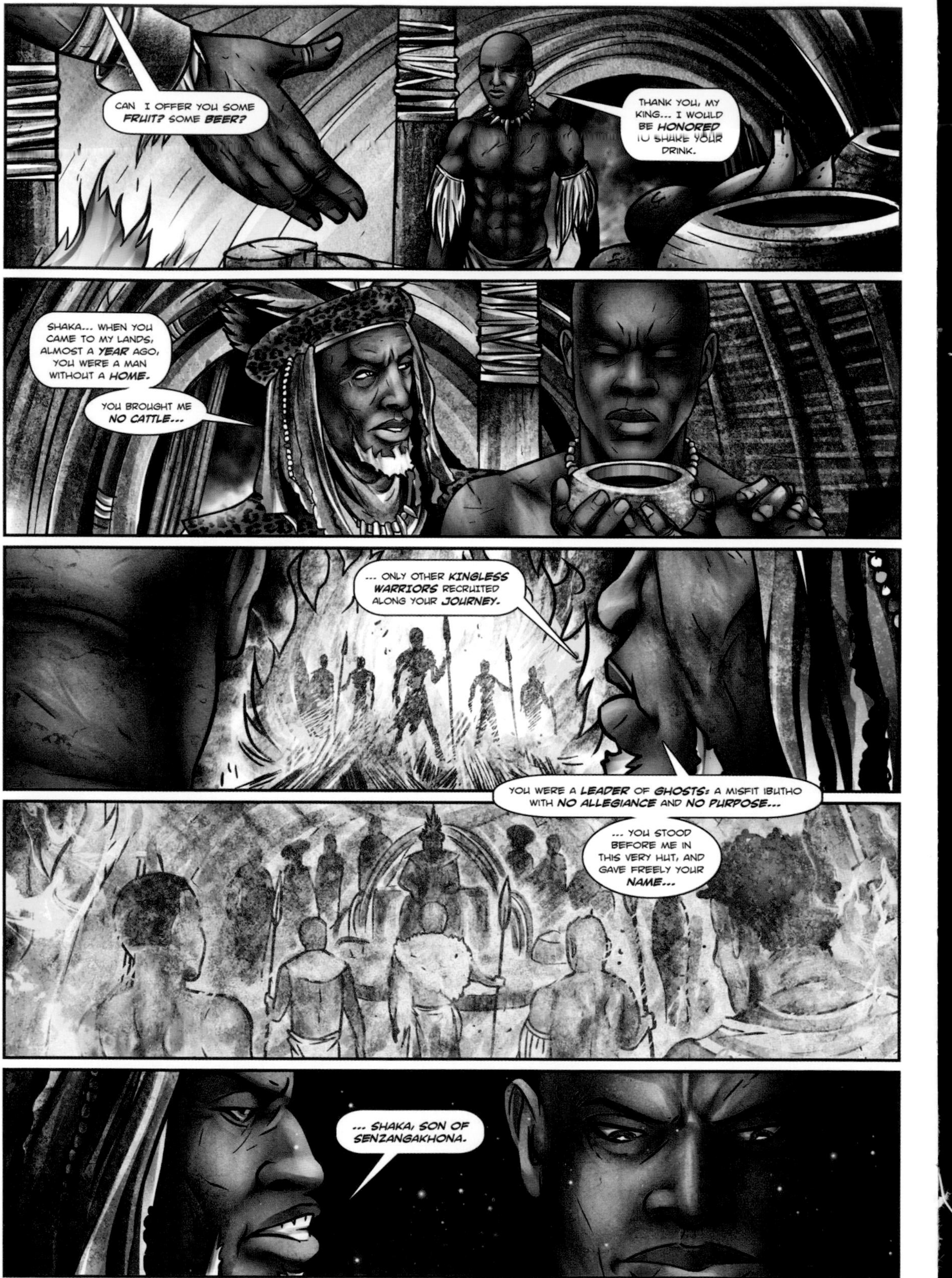
CAN I OFFER YOU SOME FRUIT? SOME BEER?
THANK YOU, MY KING... I WOULD BE HONORED TO SHARE YOUR DRINK.
SHAKA... WHEN YOU CAME TO MY LANDS, ALMOST A YEAR AGO, YOU WERE A MAN WITHOUT A HOME.
YOU BROUGHT ME NO CATTLE...
... ONLY OTHER KINGLESS WARRIORS RECRUITED ALONG YOUR JOURNEY.
YOU WERE A LEADER OF GHOSTS: A MISFIT IBUTHO WITH NO ALLEGIANCE AND NO PURPOSE...
... YOU STOOD BEFORE ME IN THIS VERY HUT, AND GAVE FREELY YOUR NAME...
... SHAKA, SON OF SENZANGAKHONA.

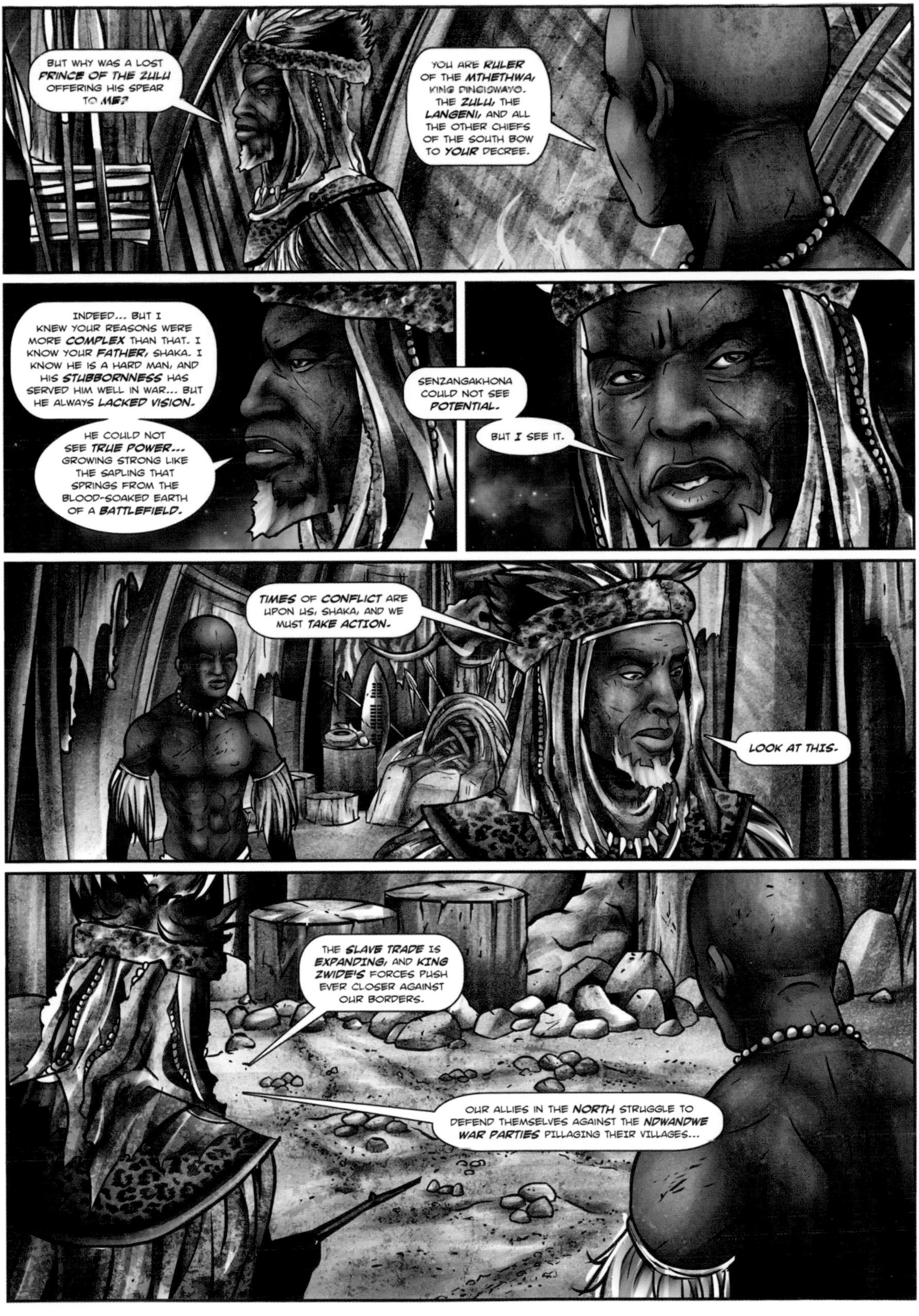
BUT WHY WAS A LOST PRINCE OF THE ZULU OFFERING HIS SPEAR TO ME?
YOU ARE RULER OF THE MTHETHWA, KING DINGISWAYO. THE ZULU, THE LANGENI, AND ALL THE OTHER CHIEFS OF THE SOUTH BOW TO YOUR DECREE.
INDEED... BUT I KNEW YOUR REASONS WERE MORE COMPLEX THAN THAT. I KNOW YOUR FATHER, SHAKA. I KNOW HE IS A HARD MAN, AND HIS STUBBORNNESS HAS SERVED HIM WELL IN WAR... BUT HE ALWAYS LACKED VISION.
HE COULD NOT SEE TRUE POWER... GROWING STRONG LIKE THE SAPLING THAT SPRINGS FROM THE BLOOD-SOAKED EARTH OF A BATTLEFIELD.
SENZANGAKHONA COULD NOT SEE POTENTIAL.
BUT I SEE IT.
TIMES OF CONFLICT ARE UPON US, SHAKA, AND WE MUST TAKE ACTION.
LOOK AT THIS.
THE SLAVE TRADE IS EXPANDING, AND KING ZWIDE'S FORCES PUSH EVER CLOSER AGAINST OUR BORDERS.
OUR ALLIES IN THE NORTH STRUGGLE TO DEFEND THEMSELVES AGAINST THE NDWANDWE WAR PARTIES PILLAGING THEIR VILLAGES...

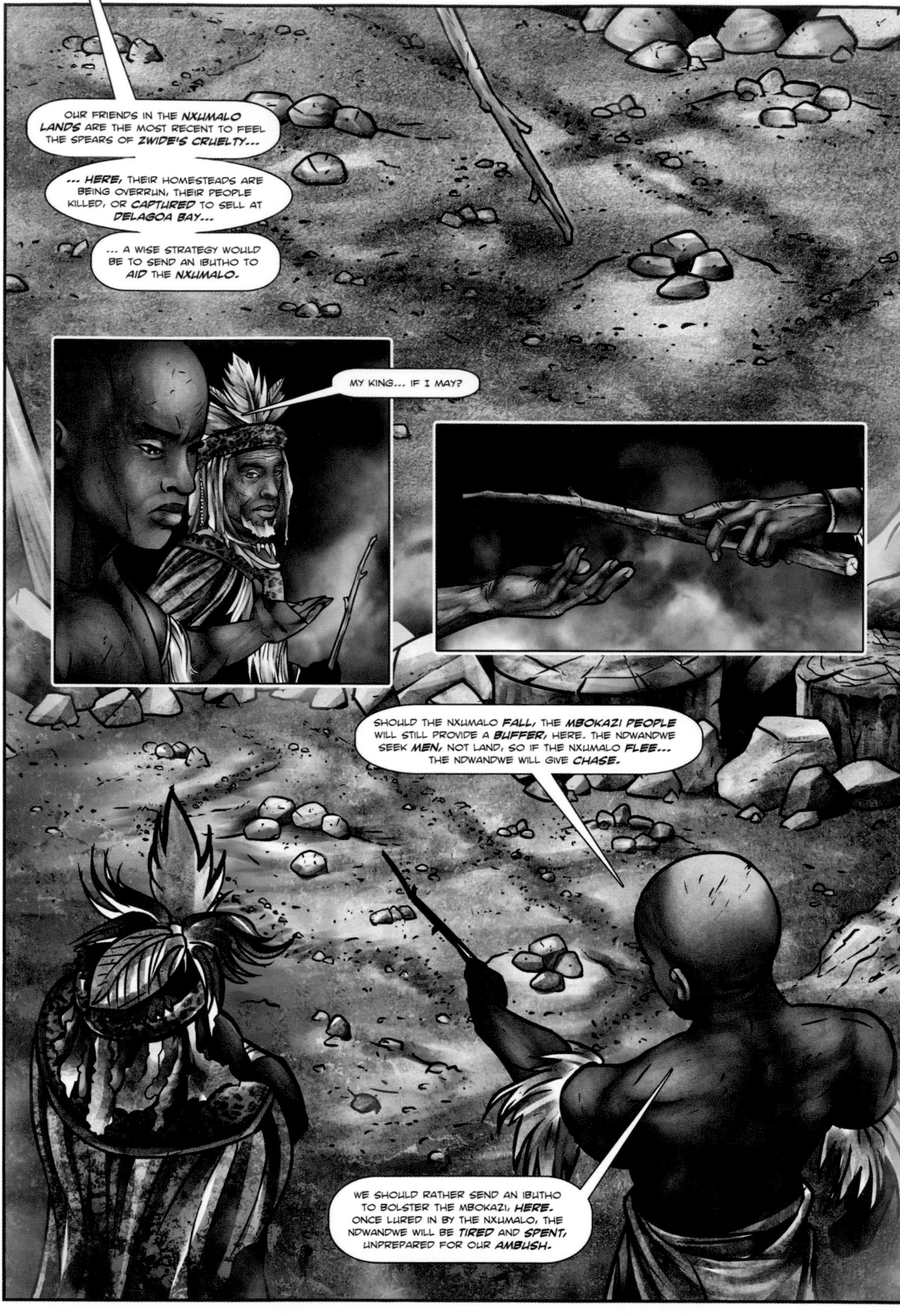
OUR FRIENDS IN THE NXUMALO LANDS ARE THE MOST RECENT TO FEEL THE SPEARS OF ZWIDE'S CRUELTY...
... HERE, THEIR HOMESTEADS ARE BEING OVERRUN, THEIR PEOPLE KILLED, OR CAPTURED TO SELL AT DELAGOA BAY...
... A WISE STRATEGY WOULD BE TO SEND AN IBUTHO TO AID THE NXUMALO.
MY KING... IF I MAY?
SHOULD THE NXUMALO FALL, THE MBOKAZI PEOPLE WILL STILL PROVIDE A BUFFER, HERE. THE NDWANDWE SEEK MEN, NOT LAND, SO IF THE NXUMALO FLEE... THE NDWANDWE WILL GIVE CHASE.
WE SHOULD RATHER SEND AN IBUTHO TO BOLSTER THE MBOKAZI, HERE. ONCE LURED IN BY THE NXUMALO, THE NDWANDWE WILL BE TIRED AND SPENT, UNPREPARED FOR OUR AMBUSH.

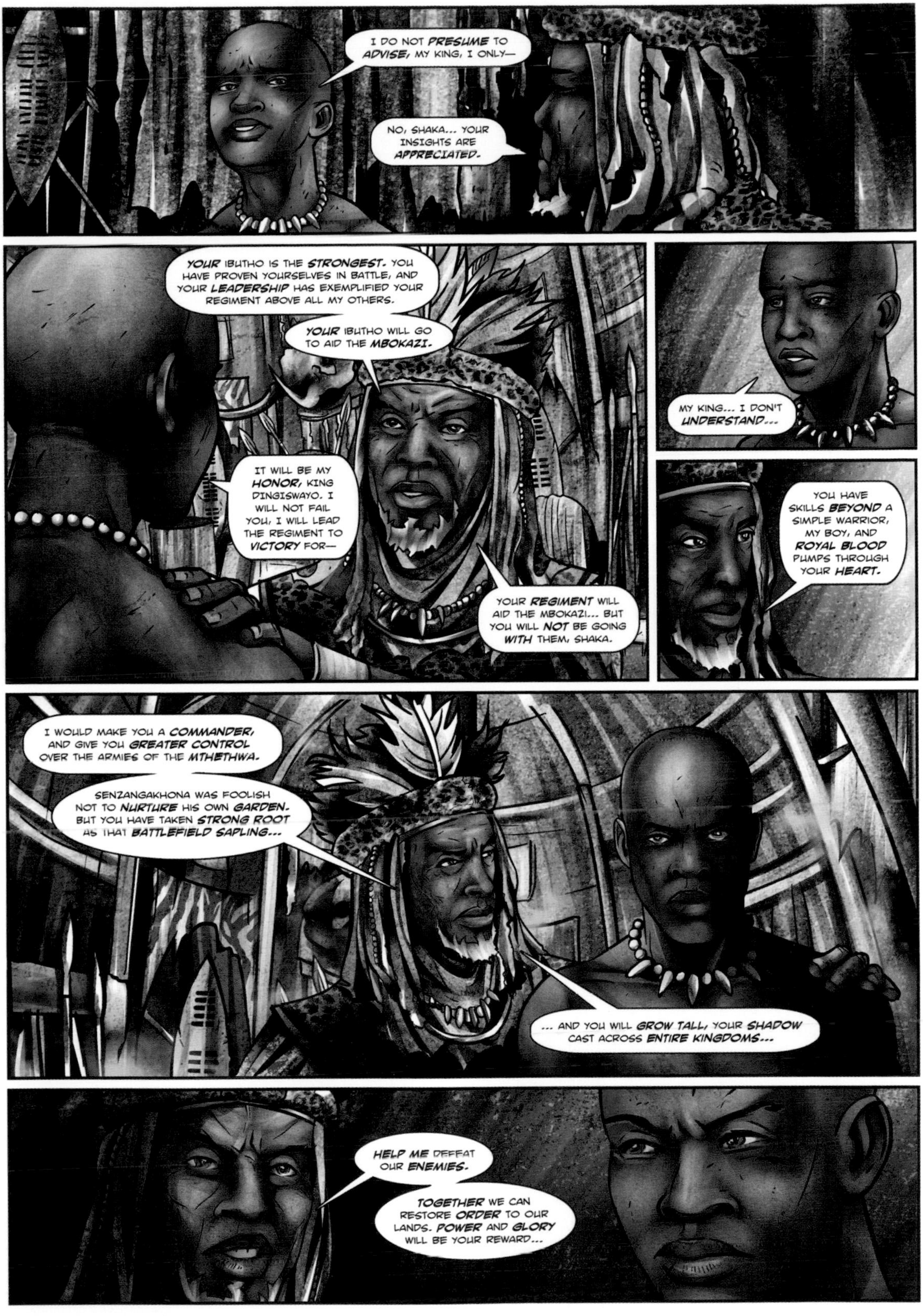
I DO NOT PRESUME TO ADVISE, MY KING, I ONLY—
NO, SHAKA... YOUR INSIGHTS ARE APPRECIATED.
YOUR IBUTHO IS THE STRONGEST. YOU HAVE PROVEN YOURSELVES IN BATTLE, AND YOUR LEADERSHIP HAS EXEMPLIFIED YOUR REGIMENT ABOVE ALL MY OTHERS.
YOUR IBUTHO WILL GO TO AID THE MBOKAZI.
IT WILL BE MY HONOR, KING DINGISWAYO. I WILL NOT FAIL YOU, I WILL LEAD THE REGIMENT TO VICTORY FOR—
YOUR REGIMENT WILL AID THE MBOKAZI... BUT YOU WILL NOT BE GOING WITH THEM, SHAKA.
MY KING... I DON'T UNDERSTAND...
YOU HAVE SKILLS BEYOND A SIMPLE WARRIOR, MY BOY, AND ROYAL BLOOD PUMPS THROUGH YOUR HEART.
I WOULD MAKE YOU A COMMANDER, AND GIVE YOU GREATER CONTROL OVER THE ARMIES OF THE MTHETHWA.
SENZANGAKHONA WAS FOOLISH NOT TO NURTURE HIS OWN GARDEN. BUT YOU HAVE TAKEN STRONG ROOT AS THAT BATTLEFIELD SAPLING...
... AND YOU WILL GROW TALL, YOUR SHADOW CAST ACROSS ENTIRE KINGDOMS...
HELP ME DEFEAT OUR ENEMIES.
TOGETHER WE CAN RESTORE ORDER TO OUR LANDS. POWER AND GLORY WILL BE YOUR REWARD...

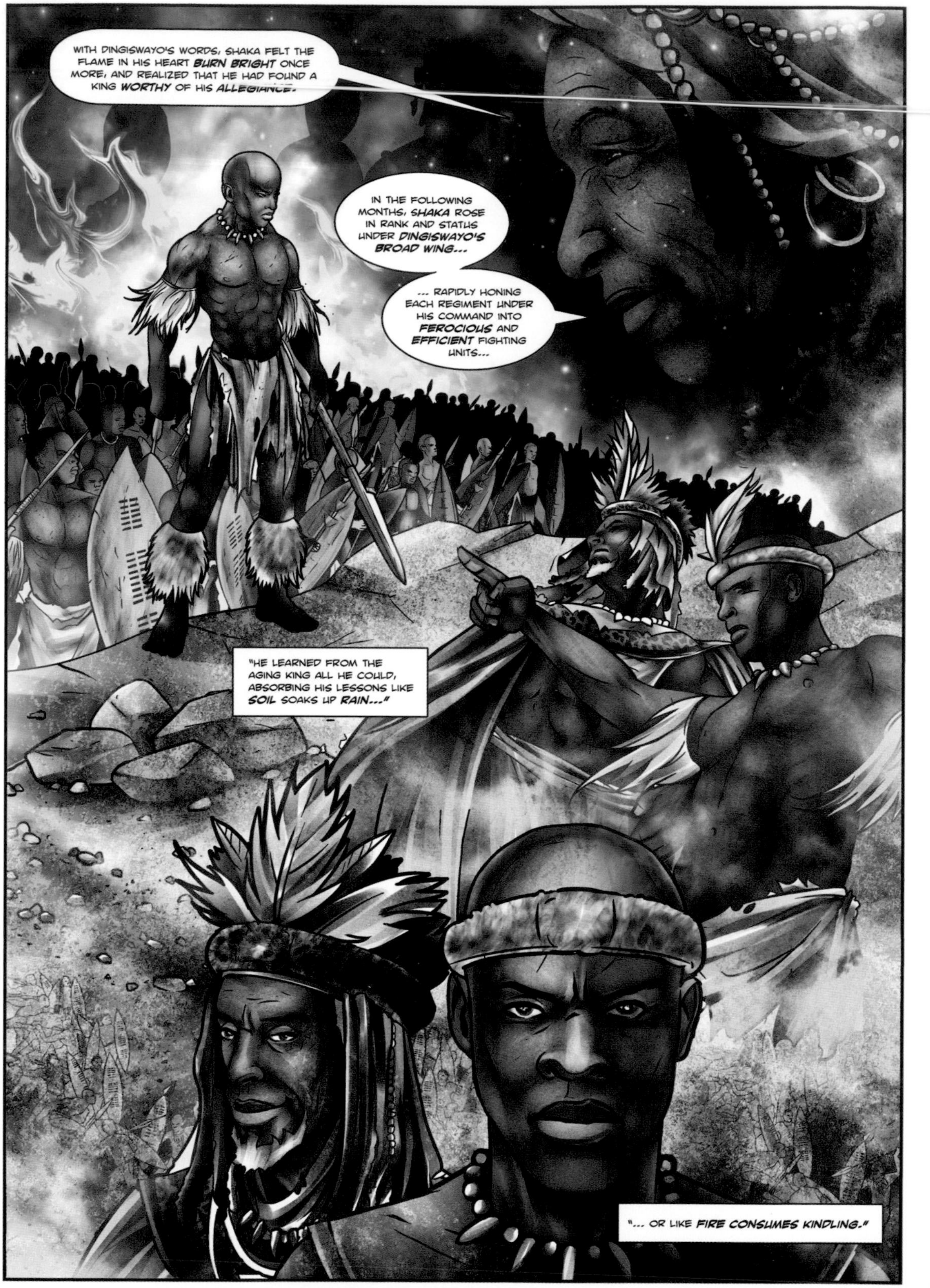
WITH DINGISWAYO'S WORDS, SHAKA FELT THE FLAME IN HIS HEART BURN BRIGHT ONCE MORE, AND REALIZED THAT HE HAD FOUND A KING WORTHY OF HIS ALLEGIANCE.
IN THE FOLLOWING MONTHS, SHAKA ROSE IN RANK AND STATUS UNDER DINGISWAYO'S BROAD WING...
... RAPIDLY HONING EACH REGIMENT UNDER HIS COMMAND INTO FEROCIOUS AND EFFICIENT FIGHTING UNITS...
"HE LEARNED FROM THE AGING KING ALL HE COULD, ABSORBING HIS LESSONS LIKE SOIL SOAKS UP RAIN..."
"... OR LIKE FIRE CONSUMES KINDLING."

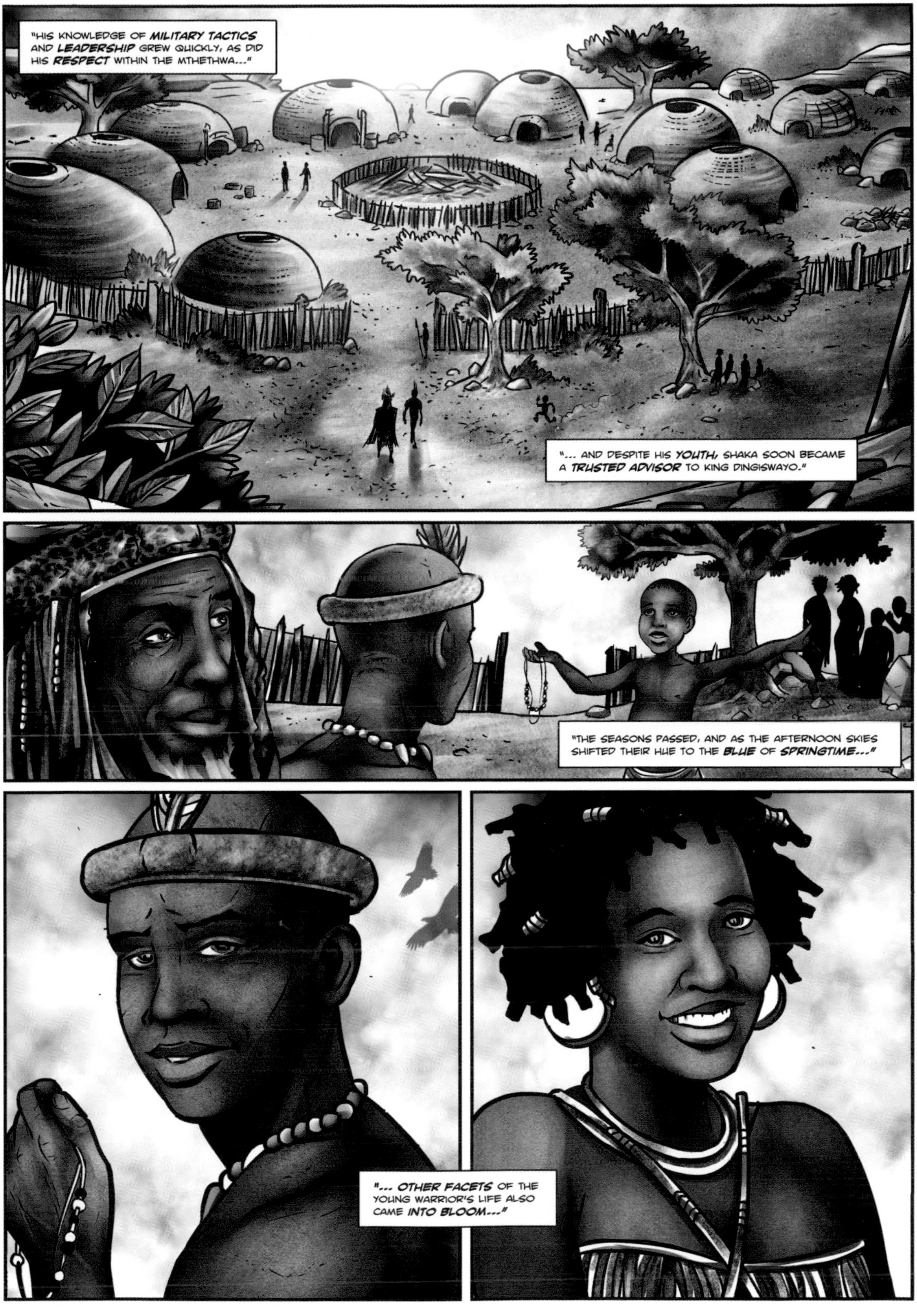
"HIS KNOWLEDGE OF MILITARY TACTICS AND LEADERSHIP GREW QUICKLY, AS DID HIS RESPECT WITHIN THE MTHETHWA..."
"... AND DESPITE HIS YOUTH, SHAKA SOON BECAME A TRUSTED ADVISOR TO KING DINGISWAYO."
"THE SEASONS PASSED, AND AS THE AFTERNOON SKIES SHIFTED THEIR HUE TO THE BLUE OF SPRINGTIME..."
"... OTHER FACETS OF THE YOUNG WARRIOR'S LIFE ALSO CAME INTO BLOOM..."

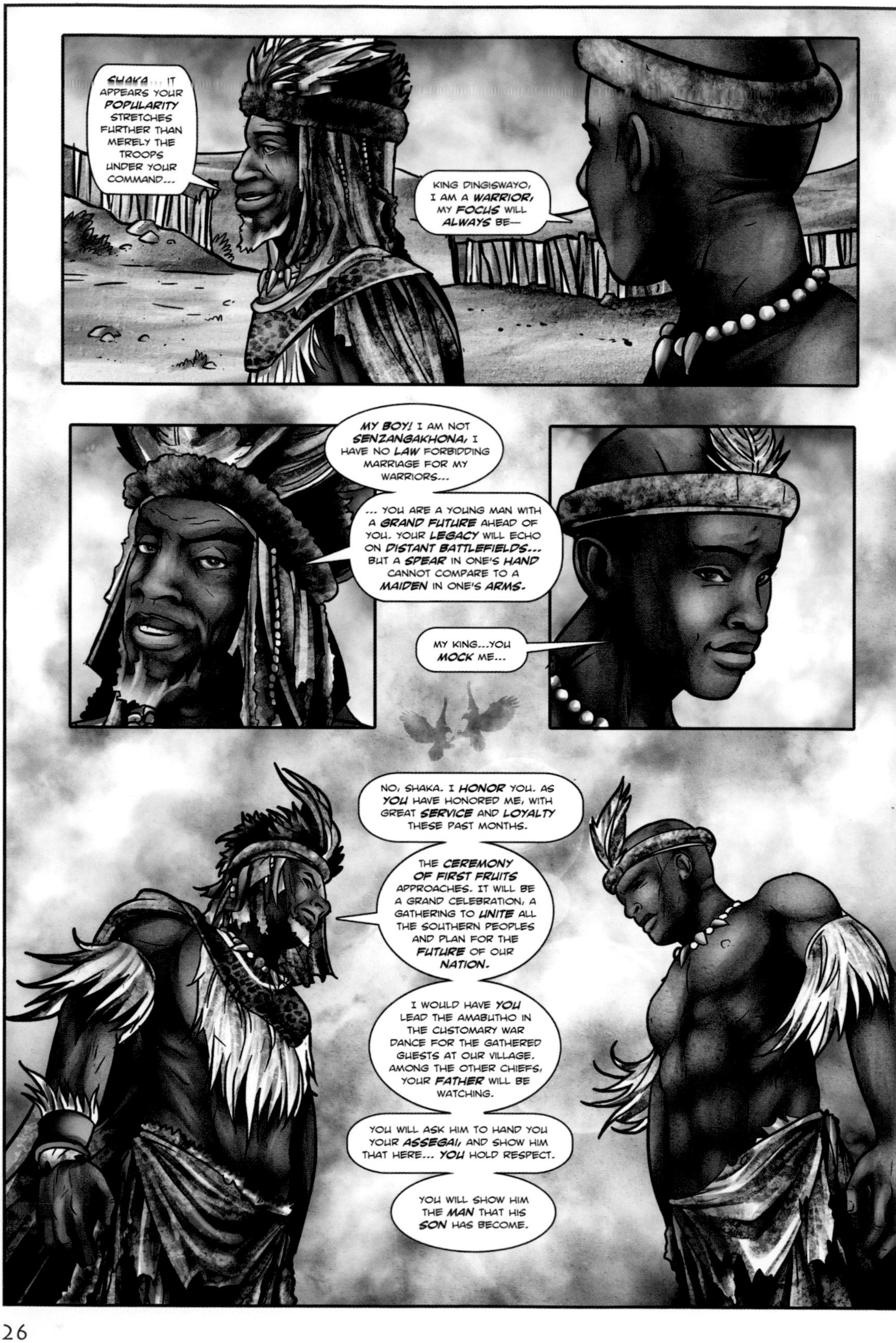
SHAKA... IT APPEARS YOUR POPULARITY STRETCHES FURTHER THAN MERELY THE TROOPS UNDER YOUR COMMAND...
KING DINGISWAYO, I AM A WARRIOR, MY FOCUS WILL ALWAYS BE—
MY BOY! I AM NOT SENZANGAKHONA, I HAVE NO LAW FORBIDDING MARRIAGE FOR MY WARRIORS...
... YOU ARE A YOUNG MAN WITH A GRAND FUTURE AHEAD OF YOU. YOUR LEGACY WILL ECHO ON DISTANT BATTLEFIELDS... BUT A SPEAR IN ONE'S HAND CANNOT COMPARE TO A MAIDEN IN ONE'S ARMS.
MY KING...YOU MOCK ME...
NO, SHAKA. I HONOR YOU. AS YOU HAVE HONORED ME, WITH GREAT SERVICE AND LOYALTY THESE PAST MONTHS.
THE CEREMONY OF FIRST FRUITS APPROACHES. IT WILL BE A GRAND CELEBRATION, A GATHERING TO UNITE ALL THE SOUTHERN PEOPLES AND PLAN FOR THE FUTURE OF OUR NATION.
I WOULD HAVE YOU LEAD THE AMABUTHO IN THE CUSTOMARY WAR DANCE FOR THE GATHERED GUESTS AT OUR VILLAGE. AMONG THE OTHER CHIEFS, YOUR FATHER WILL BE WATCHING.
YOU WILL ASK HIM TO HAND YOU YOUR ASSEGAI, AND SHOW HIM THAT HERE... YOU HOLD RESPECT.
YOU WILL SHOW HIM THE MAN THAT HIS SON HAS BECOME.

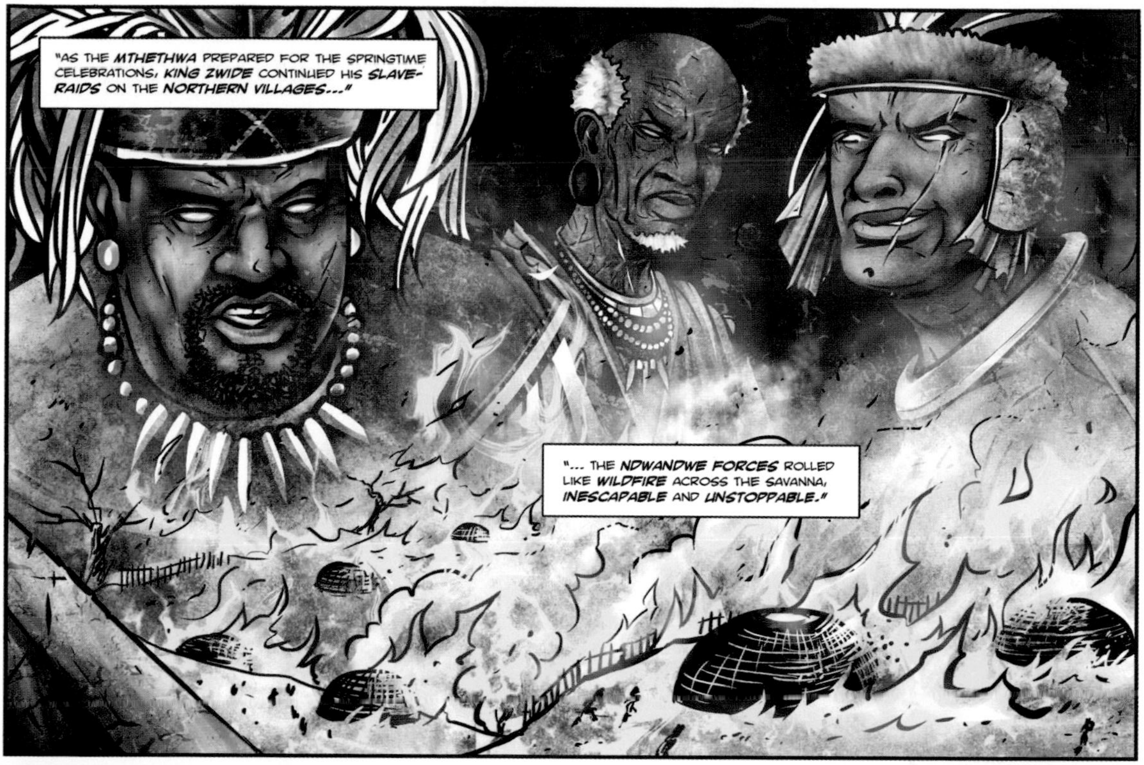
"AS THE MTHETHWA PREPARED FOR THE SPRINGTIME CELEBRATIONS, KING ZWIDE CONTINUED HIS SLAVE-RAIDS ON THE NORTHERN VILLAGES..."
"... THE NDWANDWE FORCES ROLLED LIKE WILDFIRE ACROSS THE SAVANNA, INESCAPABLE AND UNSTOPPABLE."

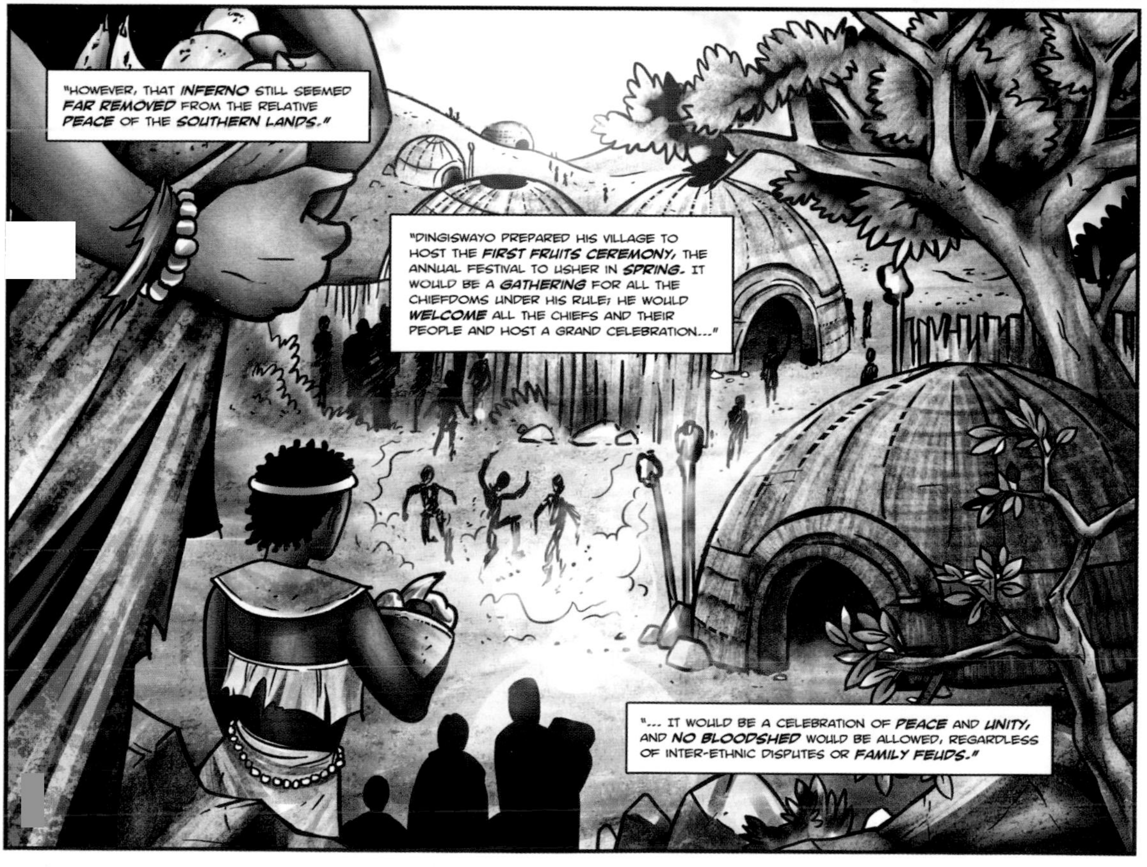
"HOWEVER, THAT INFERNO STILL SEEMED FAR REMOVED FROM THE RELATIVE PEACE OF THE SOUTHERN LANDS."
"DINGISWAYO PREPARED HIS VILLAGE TO HOST THE FIRST FRUITS CEREMONY, THE ANNUAL FESTIVAL TO USHER IN SPRING. IT WOULD BE A GATHERING FOR ALL THE CHIEFDOMS UNDER HIS RULE; HE WOULD WELCOME ALL THE CHIEFS AND THEIR PEOPLE AND HOST A GRAND CELEBRATION..."
"... IT WOULD BE A CELEBRATION OF PEACE AND UNITY, AND NO BLOODSHED WOULD BE ALLOWED, REGARDLESS OF INTER-ETHNIC DISPUTES OR FAMILY FEUDS."

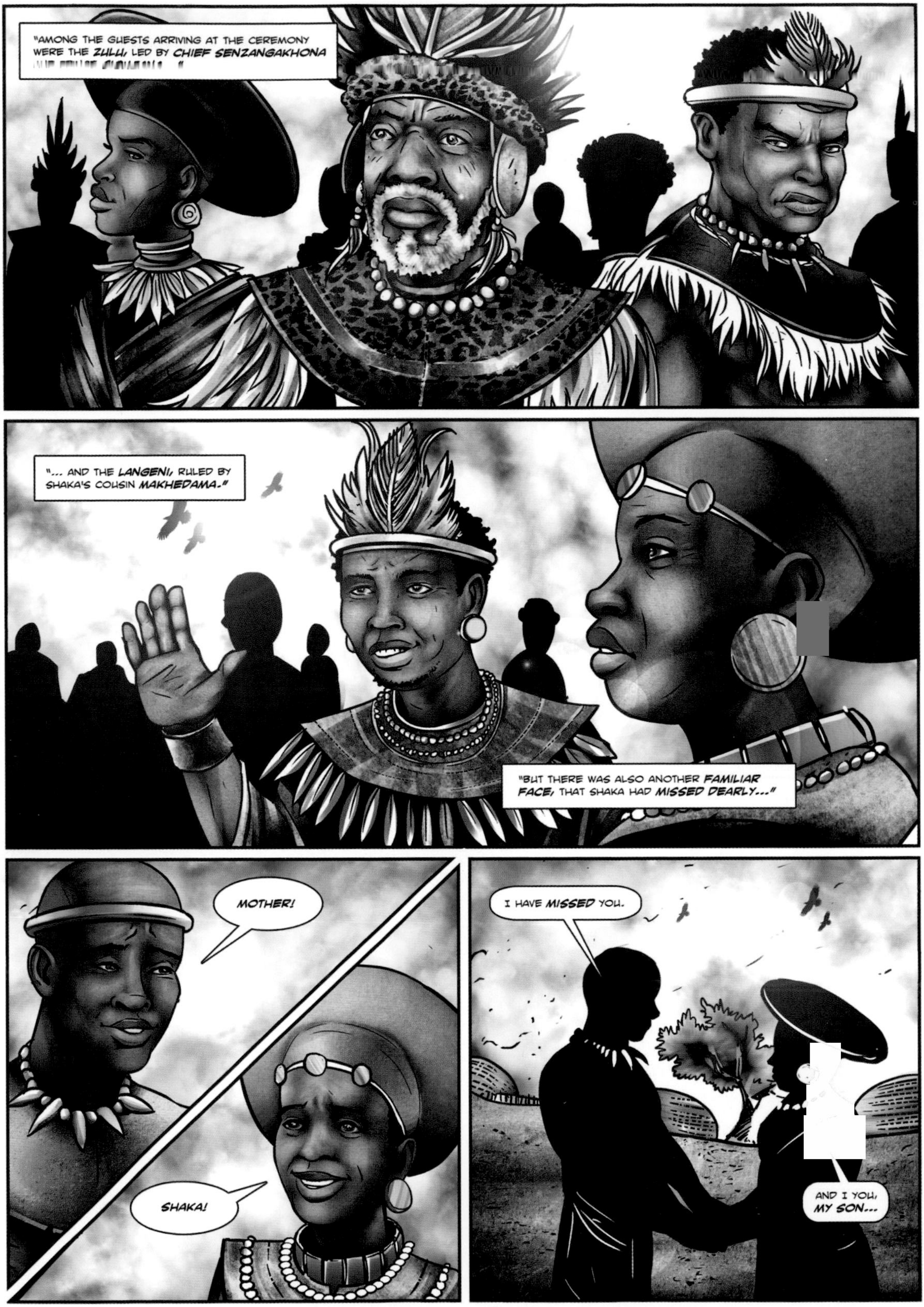
"AMONG THE GUESTS ARRIVING AT THE CEREMONY WERE THE ZULU, LED BY CHIEF SENZANGAKHONA
"... AND THE LANGENI, RULED BY SHAKA'S COUSIN MAKHEDAMA."
"BUT THERE WAS ALSO ANOTHER FAMILIAR FACE, THAT SHAKA HAD MISSED DEARLY..."
MOTHER!
SHAKA!
I HAVE MISSED YOU.
AND I YOU, MY SON...

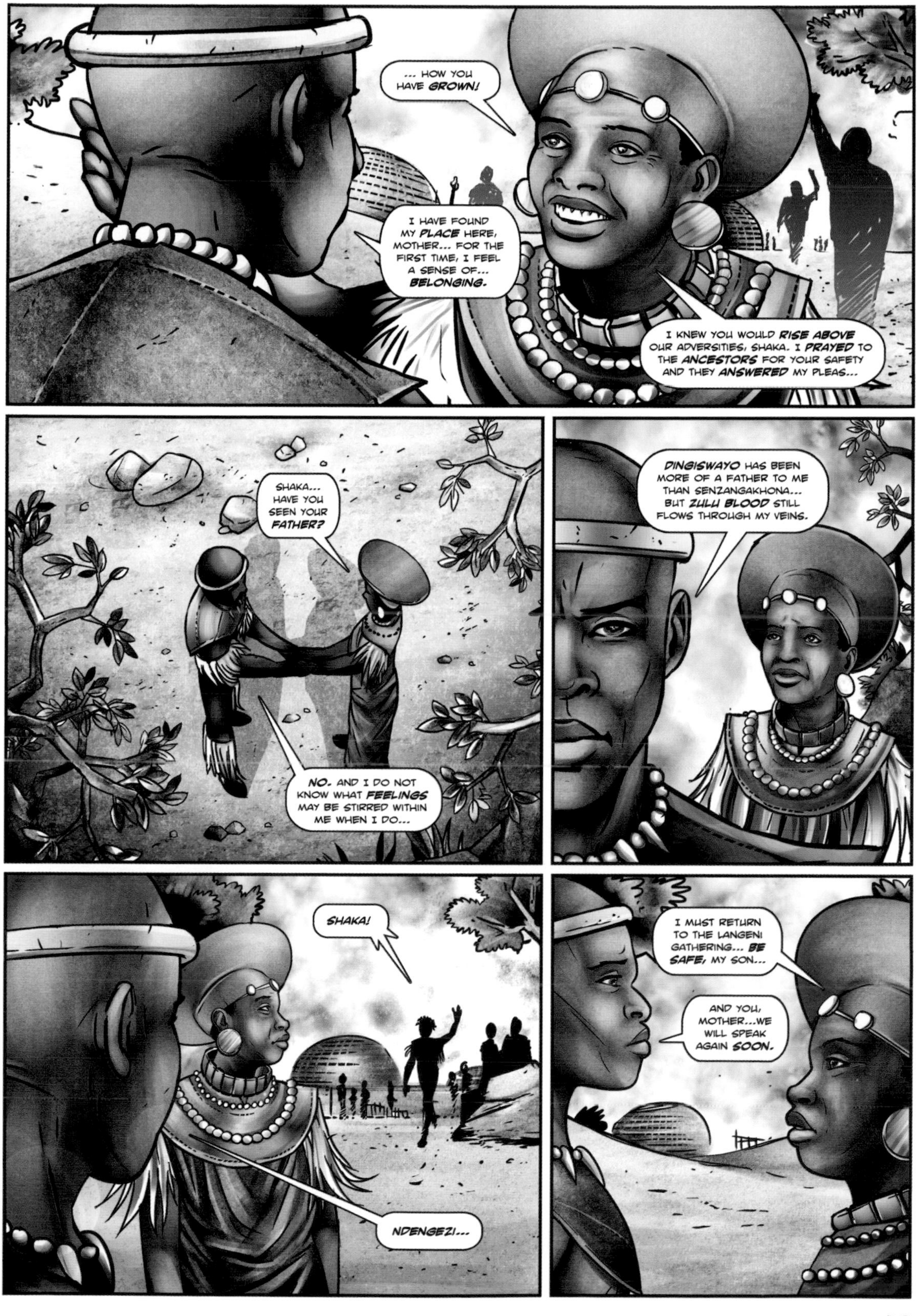
... HOW YOU HAVE GROWN!
I HAVE FOUND MY PLACE HERE, MOTHER... FOR THE FIRST TIME, I FEEL A SENSE OF... BELONGING.
I KNEW YOU WOULD RISE ABOVE OUR ADVERSITIES, SHAKA. I PRAYED TO THE ANCESTORS FOR YOUR SAFETY AND THEY ANSWERED MY PLEAS...
SHAKA... HAVE YOU SEEN YOUR FATHER?
NO. AND I DO NOT KNOW WHAT FEELINGS MAY BE STIRRED WITHIN ME WHEN I DO...
DINGISWAYO HAS BEEN MORE OF A FATHER TO ME THAN SENZANGAKHONA... BUT ZULU BLOOD STILL FLOWS THROUGH MY VEINS.
SHAKA!
NDENGEZI...
I MUST RETURN TO THE LANGENI GATHERING... BE SAFE, MY SON...
AND YOU, MOTHER...WE WILL SPEAK AGAIN SOON.

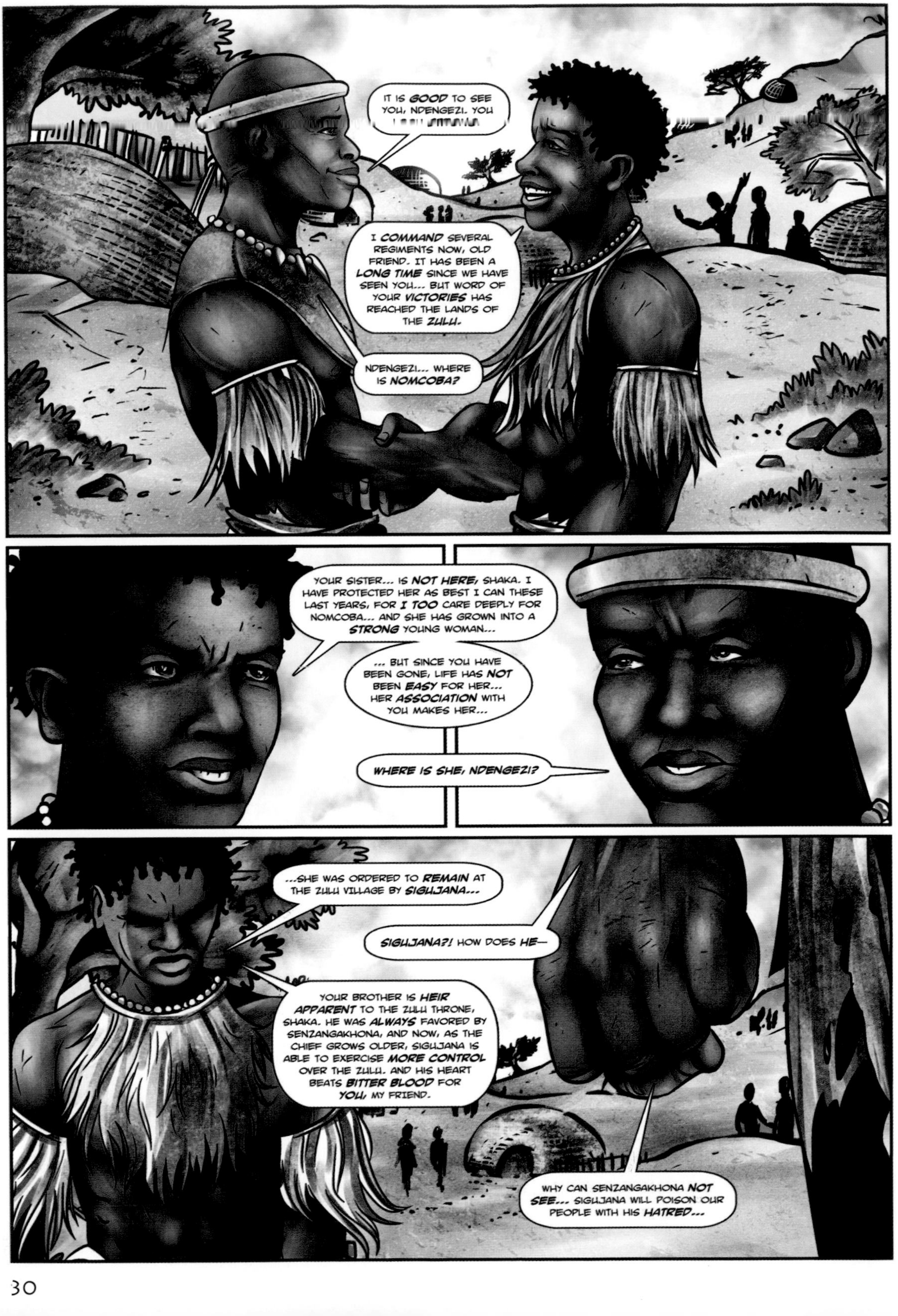
IT IS GOOD TO SEE YOU, NDENGEZI. YOU
I COMMAND SEVERAL REGIMENTS NOW, OLD FRIEND. IT HAS BEEN A LONG TIME SINCE WE HAVE SEEN YOU... BUT WORD OF YOUR VICTORIES HAS REACHED THE LANDS OF THE ZULU.
NDENGEZI... WHERE IS NOMCOBA?
YOUR SISTER... IS NOT HERE, SHAKA. I HAVE PROTECTED HER AS BEST I CAN THESE LAST YEARS, FOR I TOO CARE DEEPLY FOR NOMCOBA... AND SHE HAS GROWN INTO A STRONG YOUNG WOMAN...
... BUT SINCE YOU HAVE BEEN GONE, LIFE HAS NOT BEEN EASY FOR HER... HER ASSOCIATION WITH YOU MAKES HER...
WHERE IS SHE, NDENGEZI?
...SHE WAS ORDERED TO REMAIN AT THE ZULU VILLAGE BY SIGUJANA...
SIGUJANA?! HOW DOES HE—
YOUR BROTHER IS HEIR APPARENT TO THE ZULU THRONE, SHAKA. HE WAS ALWAYS FAVORED BY SENZANGAKHONA, AND NOW, AS THE CHIEF GROWS OLDER, SIGUJANA IS ABLE TO EXERCISE MORE CONTROL OVER THE ZULU. AND HIS HEART BEATS BITTER BLOOD FOR YOU, MY FRIEND.
WHY CAN SENZANGAKHONA NOT SEE... SIGUJANA WILL POISON OUR PEOPLE WITH HIS HATRED...

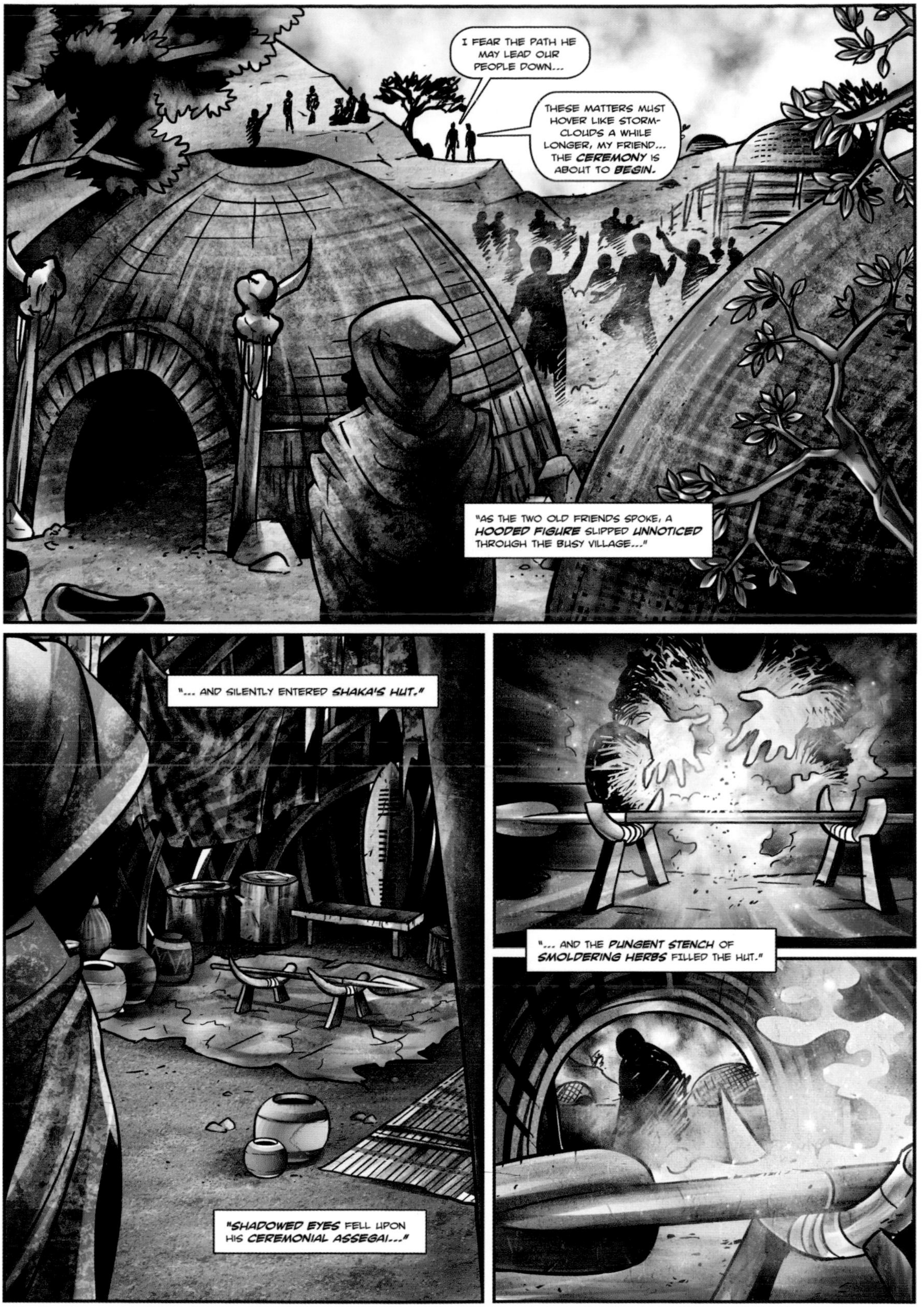
I FEAR THE PATH HE MAY LEAD OUR PEOPLE DOWN...
THESE MATTERS MUST HOVER LIKE STORM-CLOUDS A WHILE LONGER, MY FRIEND... THE CEREMONY IS ABOUT TO BEGIN.
"AS THE TWO OLD FRIENDS SPOKE, A HOODED FIGURE SLIPPED UNNOTICED THROUGH THE BUSY VILLAGE..."
"... AND SILENTLY ENTERED SHAKA'S HUT."
"SHADOWED EYES FELL UPON HIS CEREMONIAL ASSEGAI..."
"... AND THE PUNGENT STENCH OF SMOLDERING HERBS FILLED THE HUT."

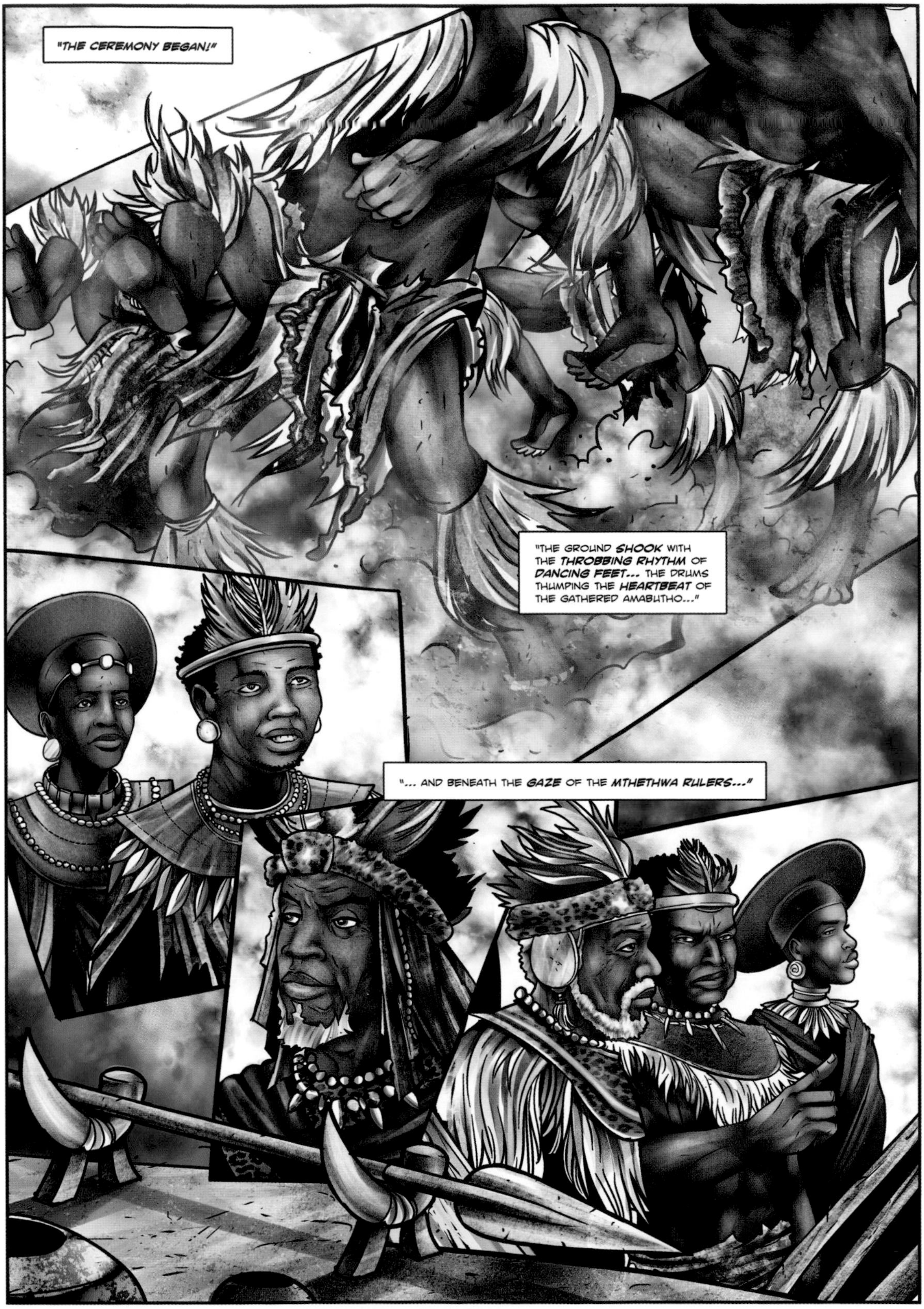
"THE CEREMONY BEGAN!"
"THE GROUND SHOOK WITH THE THROBBING RHYTHM OF DANCING FEET... THE DRUMS THUMPING THE HEARTBEAT OF THE GATHERED AMABUTHO..."
"... AND BENEATH THE GAZE OF THE MTHETHWA RULERS..."

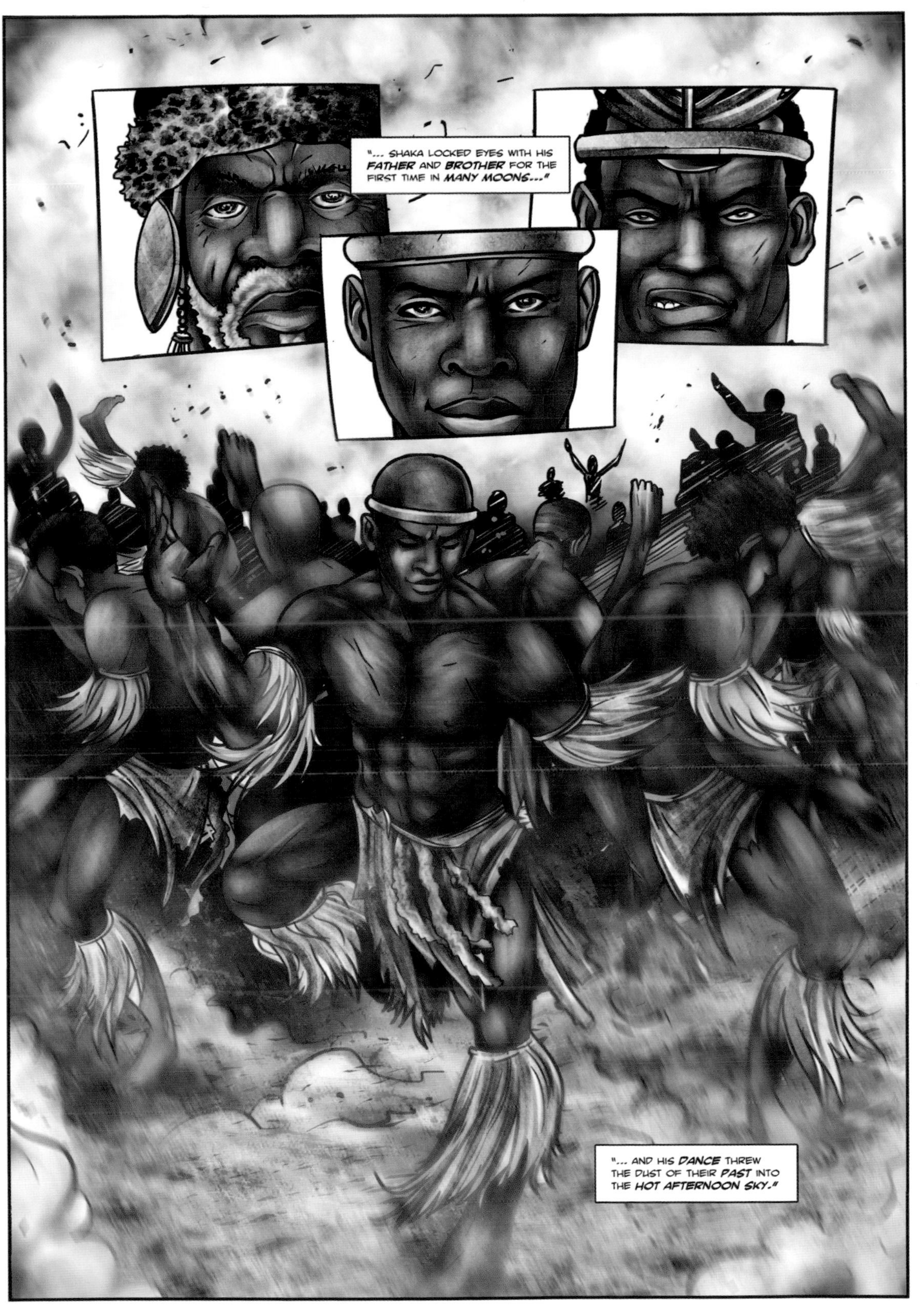
"... SHAKA LOCKED EYES WITH HIS FATHER AND BROTHER FOR THE FIRST TIME IN MANY MOONS..."
"... AND HIS DANCE THREW THE DUST OF THEIR PAST INTO THE HOT AFTERNOON SKY."

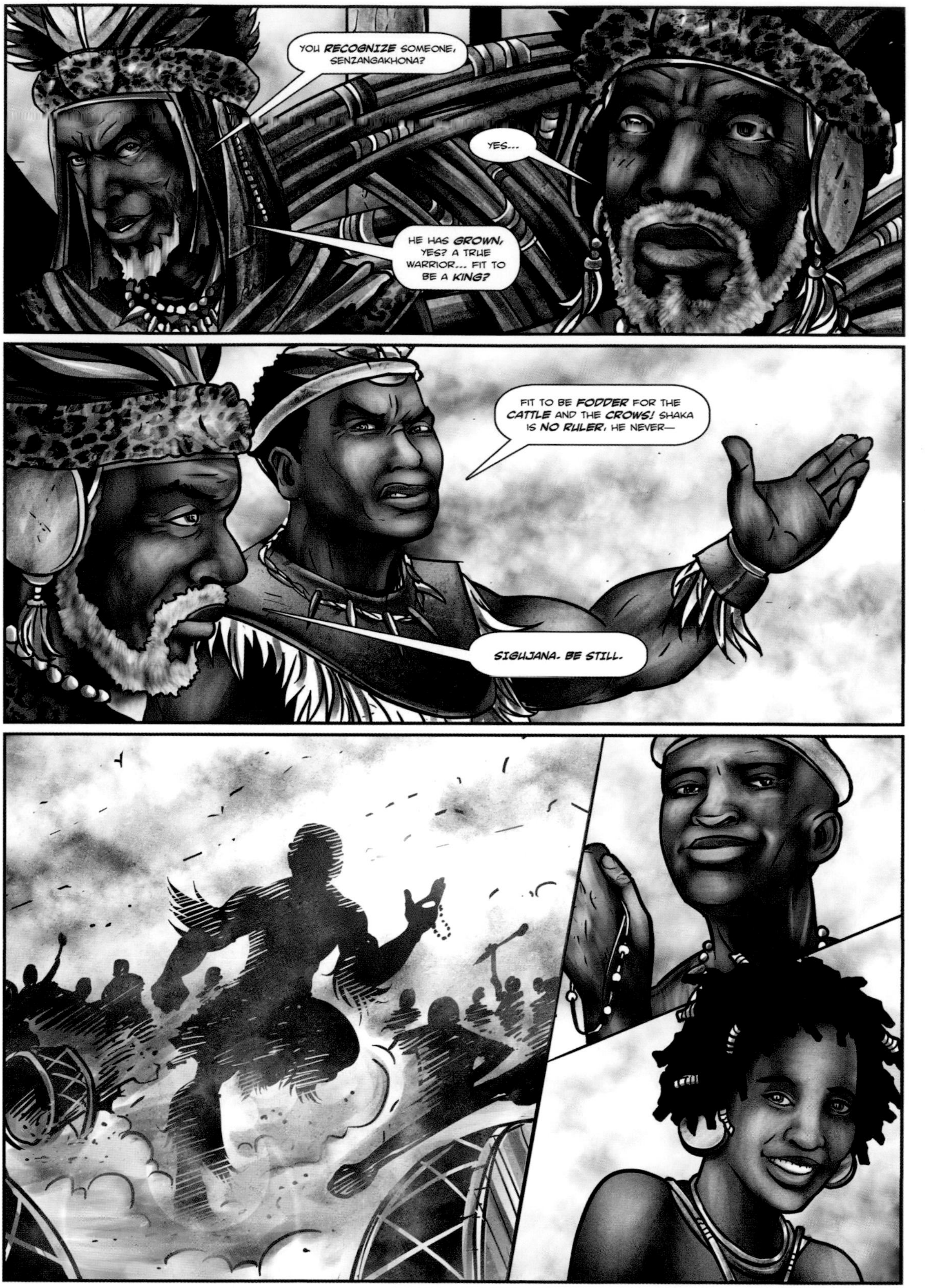
YOU RECOGNIZE SOMEONE, SENZANGAKHONA?
YES...
HE HAS GROWN, YES? A TRUE WARRIOR... FIT TO BE A KING?
FIT TO BE FODDER FOR THE CATTLE AND THE CROWS! SHAKA IS NO RULER. HE NEVER—
SIGUJANA. BE STILL.

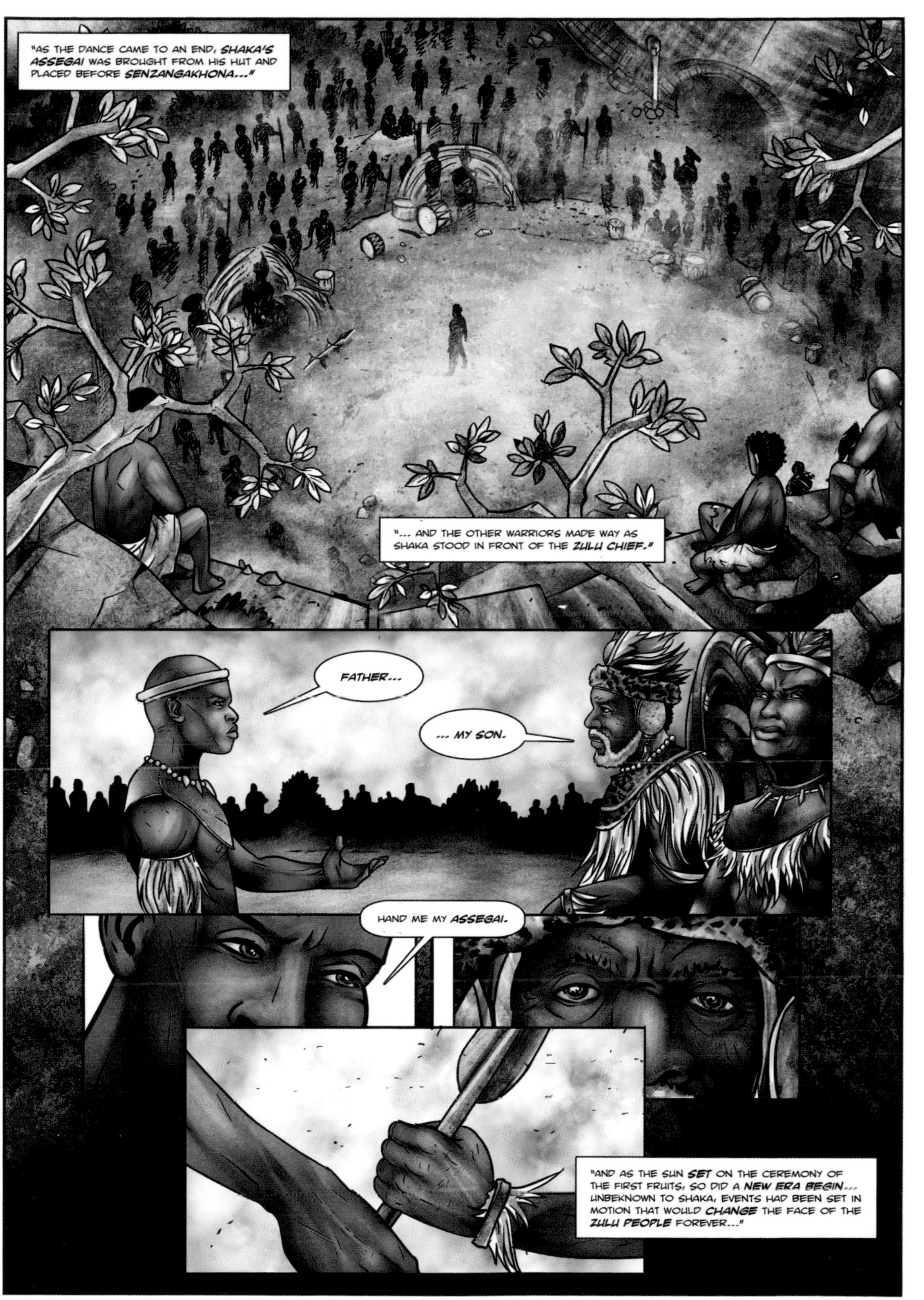
"AS THE DANCE CAME TO AN END, SHAKA'S ASSEGAI WAS BROUGHT FROM HIS HUT AND PLACED BEFORE SENZANGAKHONA..."
"... AND THE OTHER WARRIORS MADE WAY AS SHAKA STOOD IN FRONT OF THE ZULU CHIEF."
FATHER...
... MY SON.
HAND ME MY ASSEGAI.
"AND AS THE SUN SET ON THE CEREMONY OF THE FIRST FRUITS, SO DID A NEW ERA BEGIN... UNBEKNOWN TO SHAKA, EVENTS HAD BEEN SET IN MOTION THAT WOULD CHANGE THE FACE OF THE ZULU PEOPLE FOREVER..."

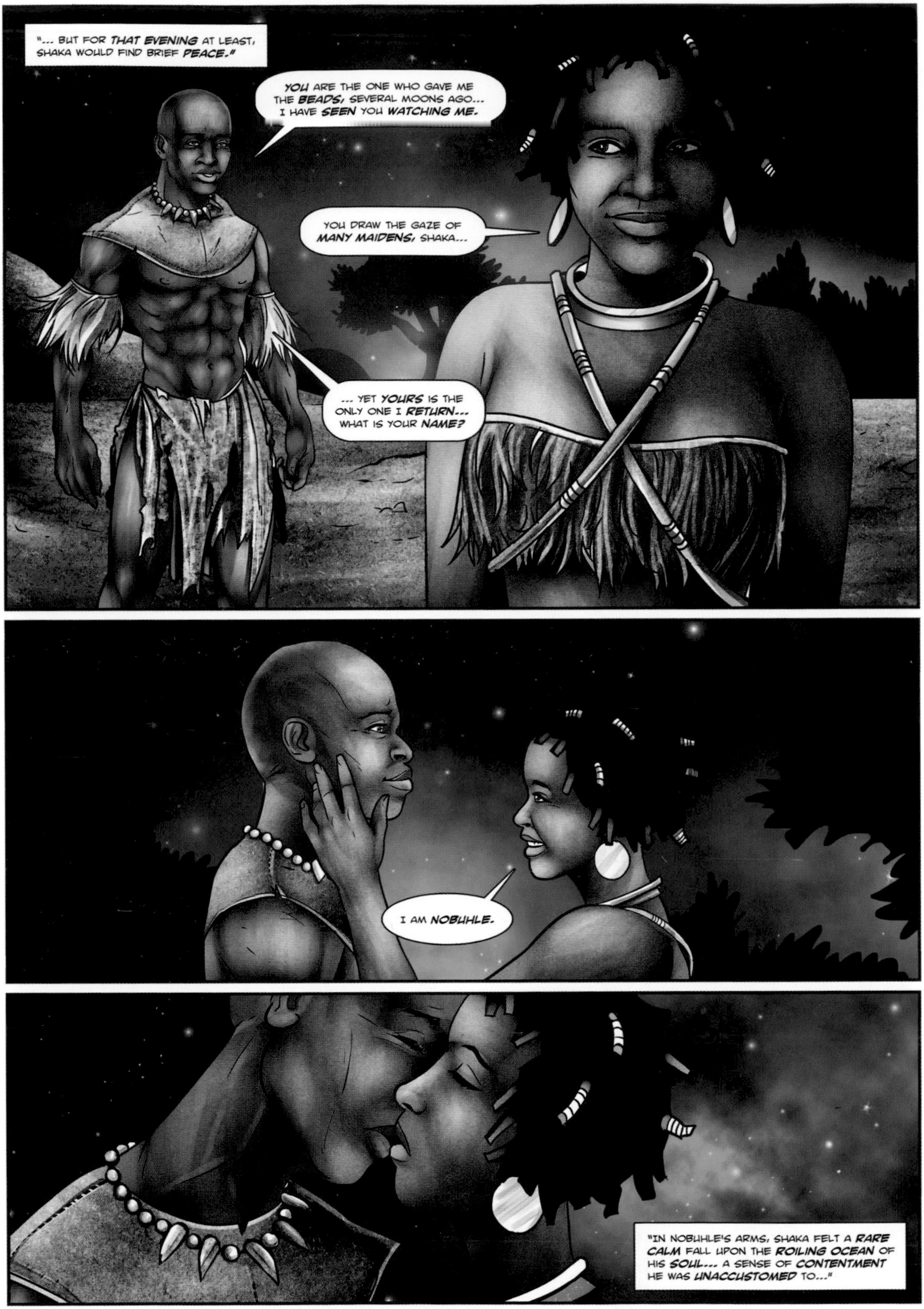
"... BUT FOR THAT EVENING AT LEAST, SHAKA WOULD FIND BRIEF PEACE."
YOU ARE THE ONE WHO GAVE ME THE BEADS, SEVERAL MOONS AGO... I HAVE SEEN YOU WATCHING ME.
YOU DRAW THE GAZE OF MANY MAIDENS, SHAKA...
... YET YOURS IS THE ONLY ONE I RETURN... WHAT IS YOUR NAME?
I AM NOBUHLE.
"IN NOBUHLE'S ARMS, SHAKA FELT A RARE CALM FALL UPON THE ROILING OCEAN OF HIS SOUL... A SENSE OF CONTENTMENT HE WAS UNACCUSTOMED TO..."

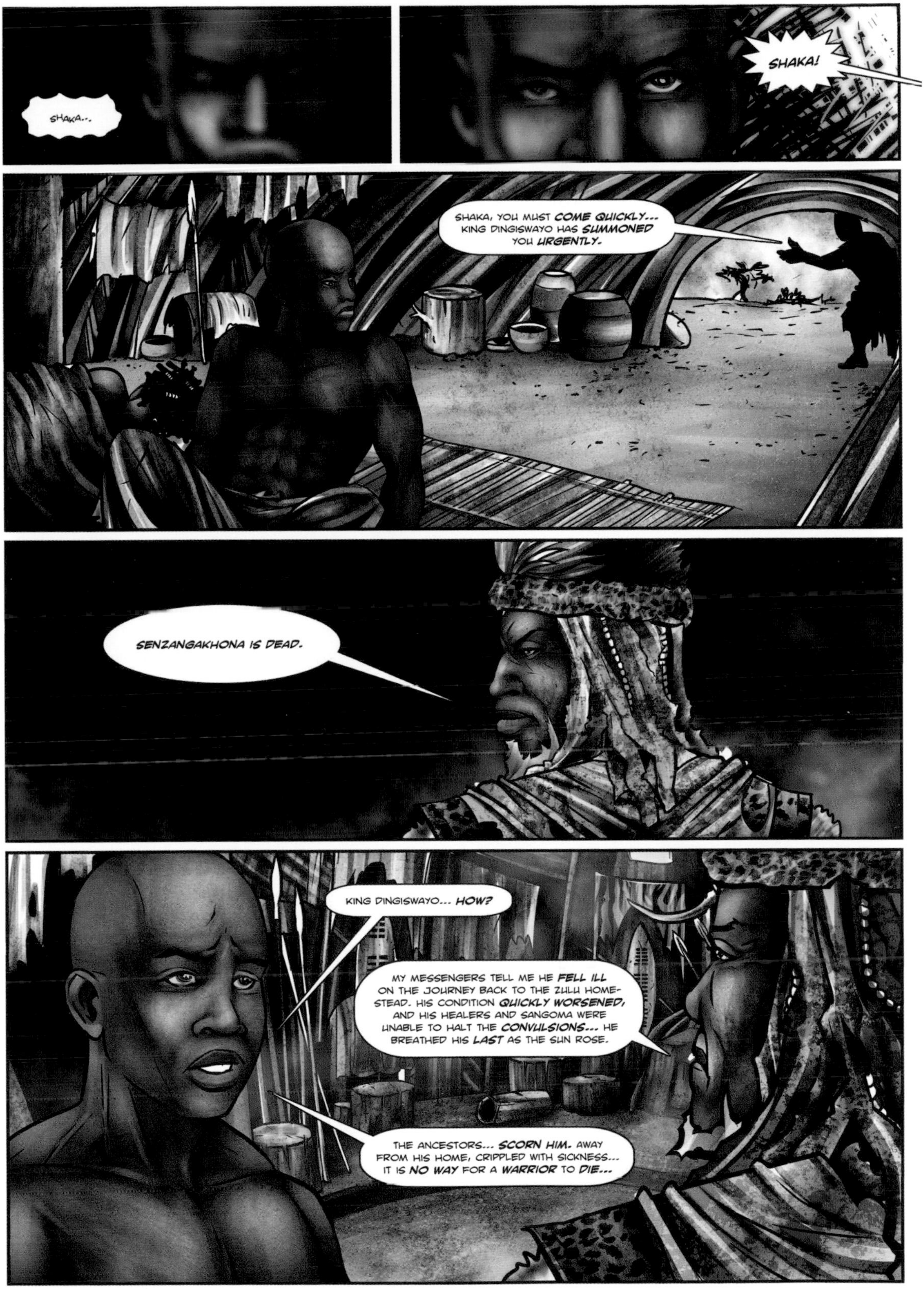
SHAKA...
SHAKA!
SHAKA, YOU MUST COME QUICKLY... KING DINGISWAYO HAS SUMMONED YOU URGENTLY.
SENZANGAKHONA IS DEAD.
KING DINGISWAYO... HOW?
MY MESSENGERS TELL ME HE FELL ILL ON THE JOURNEY BACK TO THE ZULU HOME-STEAD. HIS CONDITION QUICKLY WORSENED, AND HIS HEALERS AND SANGOMA WERE UNABLE TO HALT THE CONVULSIONS... HE BREATHED HIS LAST AS THE SUN ROSE.
THE ANCESTORS... SCORN HIM. AWAY FROM HIS HOME, CRIPPLED WITH SICKNESS... IT IS NO WAY FOR A WARRIOR TO DIE...

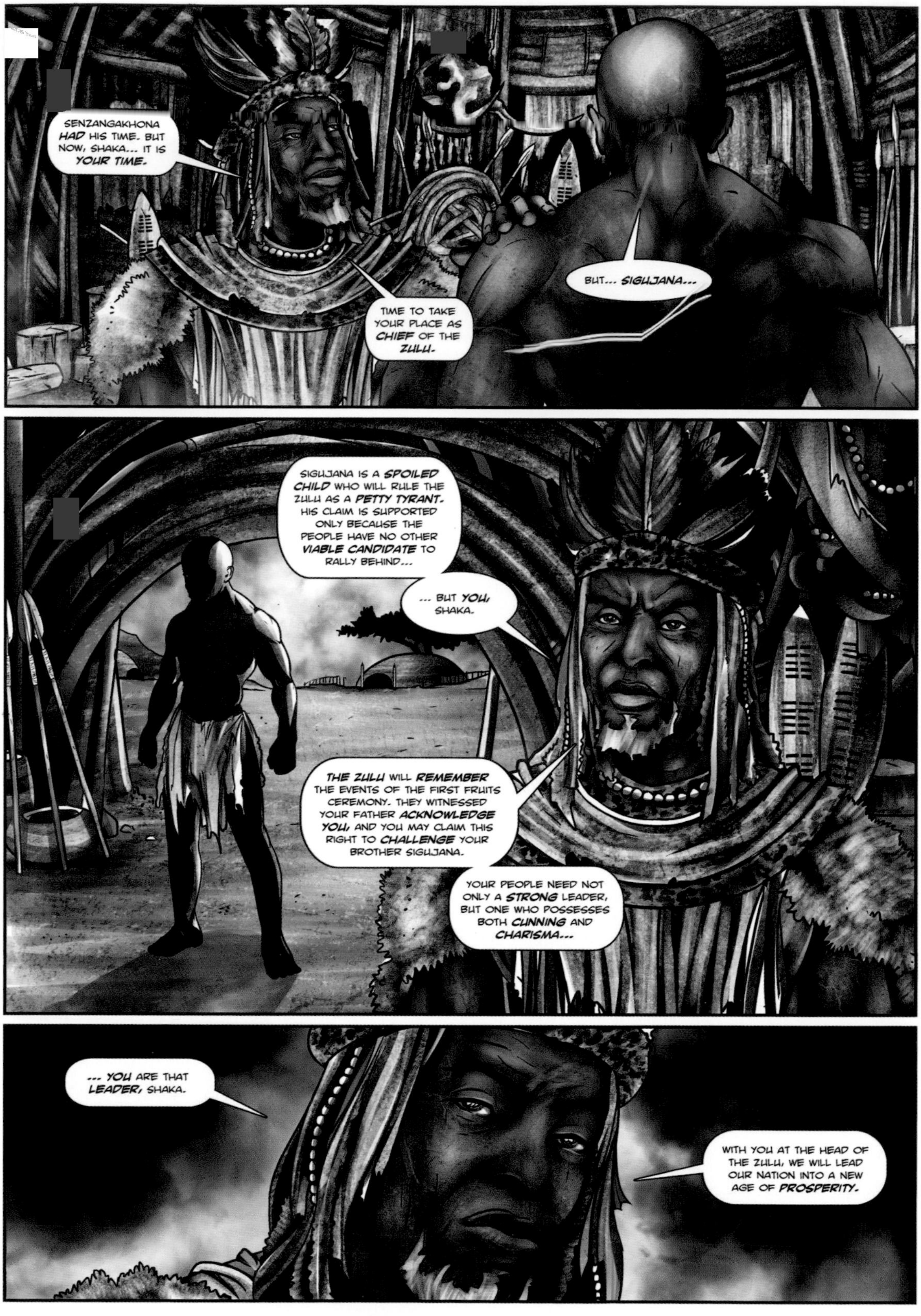
SENZANGAKHONA HAD HIS TIME. BUT NOW, SHAKA... IT IS YOUR TIME.
TIME TO TAKE YOUR PLACE AS CHIEF OF THE ZULU.
BUT... SIGUJANA...
SIGUJANA IS A SPOILED CHILD WHO WILL RULE THE ZULU AS A PETTY TYRANT. HIS CLAIM IS SUPPORTED ONLY BECAUSE THE PEOPLE HAVE NO OTHER VIABLE CANDIDATE TO RALLY BEHIND...
... BUT YOU, SHAKA.
THE ZULU WILL REMEMBER THE EVENTS OF THE FIRST FRUITS CEREMONY. THEY WITNESSED YOUR FATHER ACKNOWLEDGE YOU, AND YOU MAY CLAIM THIS RIGHT TO CHALLENGE YOUR BROTHER SIGUJANA.
YOUR PEOPLE NEED NOT ONLY A STRONG LEADER, BUT ONE WHO POSSESSES BOTH CUNNING AND CHARISMA...
... YOU ARE THAT LEADER, SHAKA.
WITH YOU AT THE HEAD OF THE ZULU, WE WILL LEAD OUR NATION INTO A NEW AGE OF PROSPERITY.

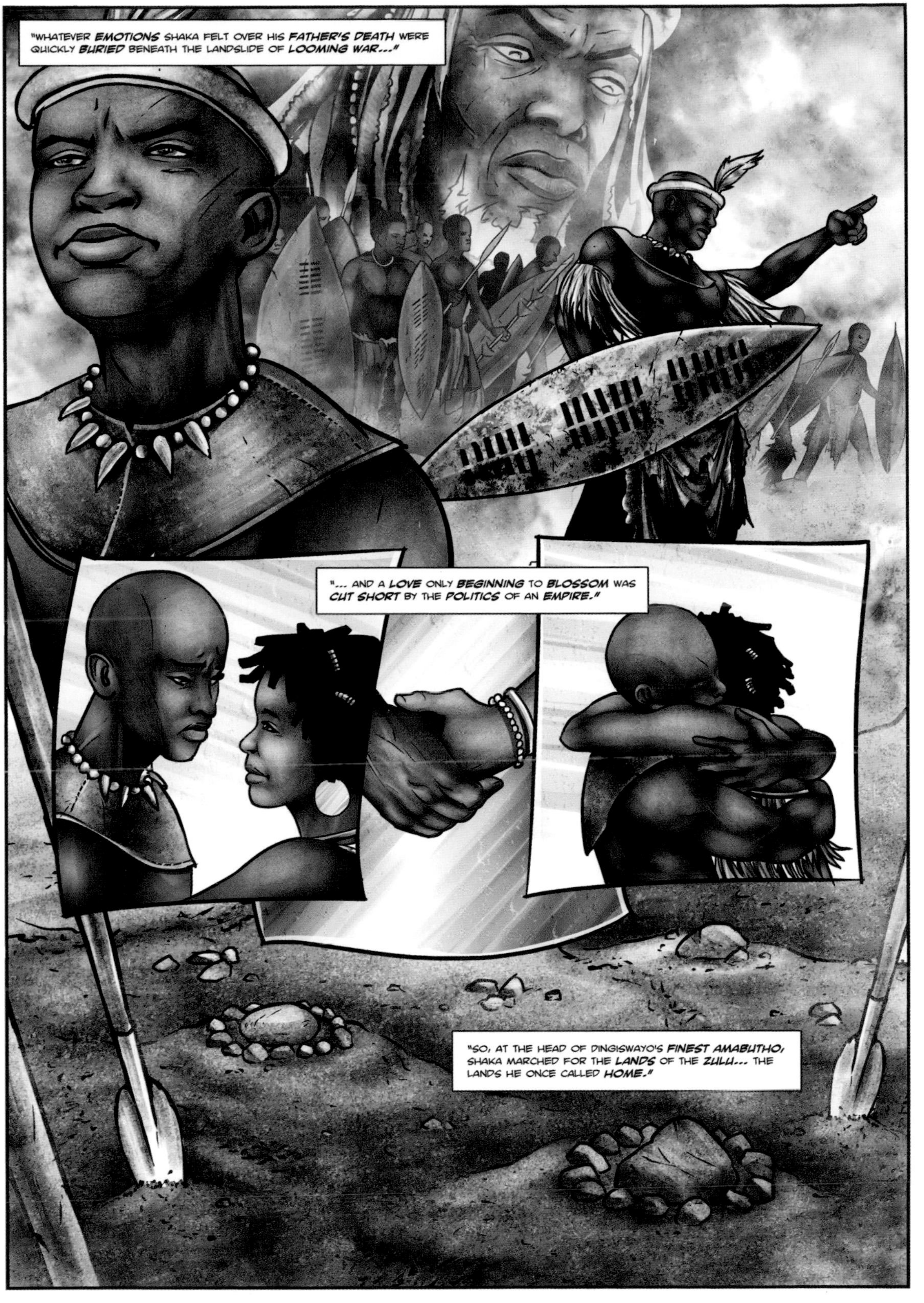
"WHATEVER EMOTIONS SHAKA FELT OVER HIS FATHER'S DEATH WERE QUICKLY BURIED BENEATH THE LANDSLIDE OF LOOMING WAR..."
"... AND A LOVE ONLY BEGINNING TO BLOSSOM WAS CUT SHORT BY THE POLITICS OF AN EMPIRE."
"SO, AT THE HEAD OF DINGISWAYO'S FINEST AMABUTHO, SHAKA MARCHED FOR THE LANDS OF THE ZULU... THE LANDS HE ONCE CALLED HOME."

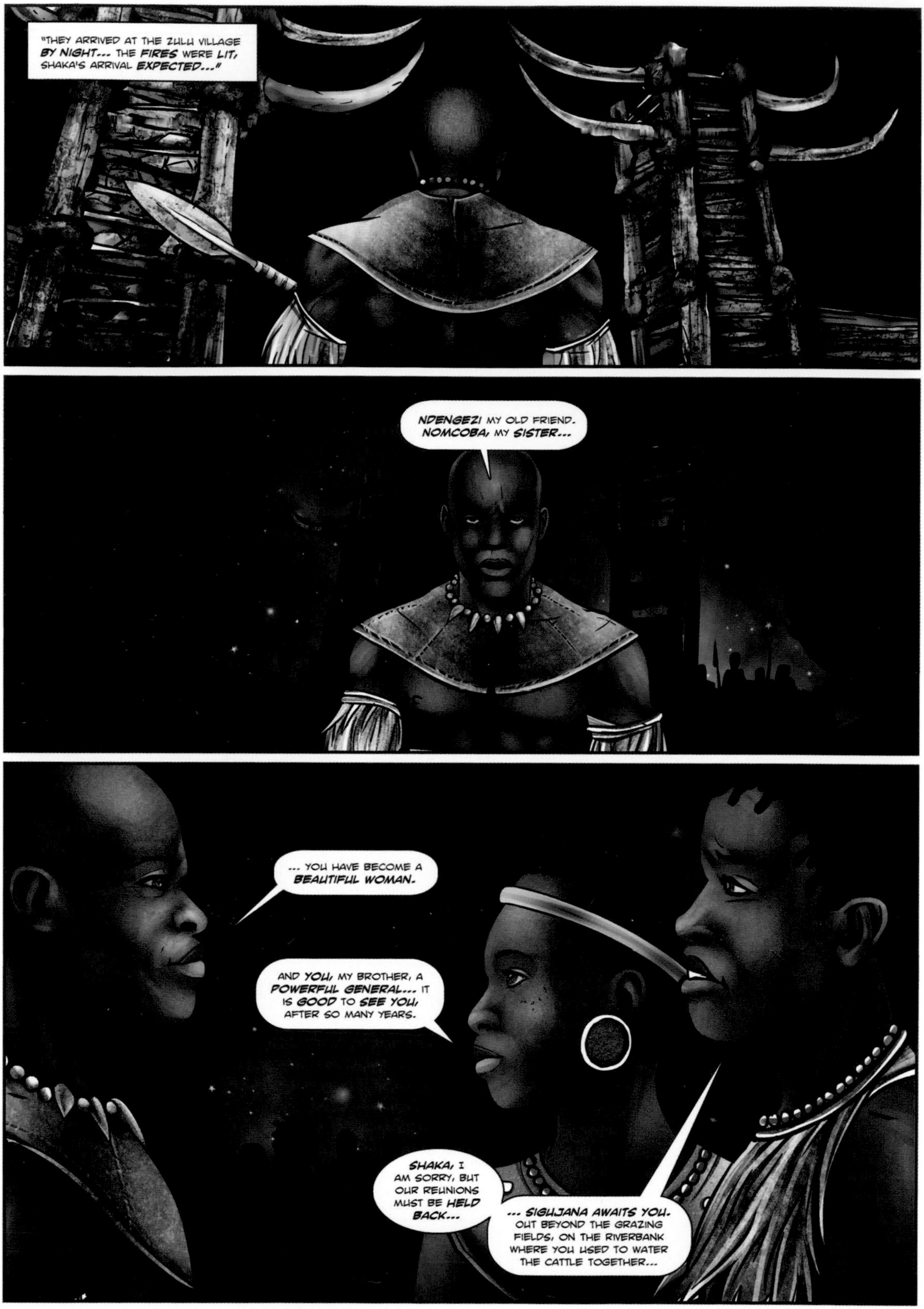
"THEY ARRIVED AT THE ZULU VILLAGE BY NIGHT... THE FIRES WERE LIT, SHAKA'S ARRIVAL EXPECTED..."
NDENGEZI MY OLD FRIEND. NOMCOBA, MY SISTER...
... YOU HAVE BECOME A BEAUTIFUL WOMAN.
AND YOU, MY BROTHER, A POWERFUL GENERAL... IT IS GOOD TO SEE YOU, AFTER SO MANY YEARS.
SHAKA, I AM SORRY, BUT OUR REUNIONS MUST BE HELD BACK...
... SIGUJANA AWAITS YOU. OUT BEYOND THE GRAZING FIELDS, ON THE RIVERBANK WHERE YOU USED TO WATER THE CATTLE TOGETHER...

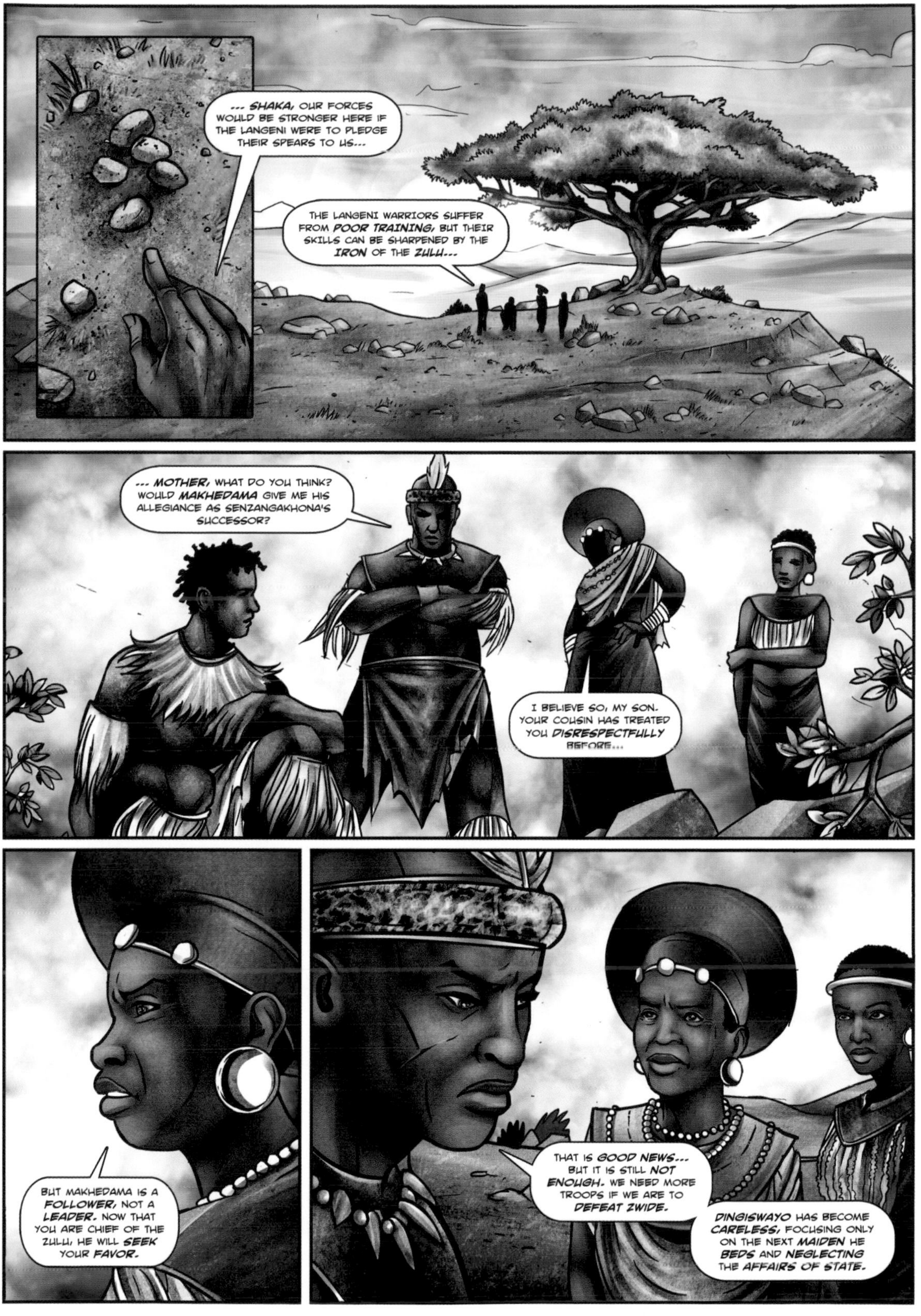
... SHAKA, OUR FORCES WOULD BE STRONGER HERE IF THE LANGENI WERE TO PLEDGE THEIR SPEARS TO US...
THE LANGENI WARRIORS SUFFER FROM POOR TRAINING, BUT THEIR SKILLS CAN BE SHARPENED BY THE IRON OF THE ZULU...
... MOTHER, WHAT DO YOU THINK? WOULD MAKHEDAMA GIVE ME HIS ALLEGIANCE AS SENZANGAKHONA'S SUCCESSOR?
I BELIEVE SO, MY SON. YOUR COUSIN HAS TREATED YOU DISRESPECTFULLY BEFORE...
BUT MAKHEDAMA IS A FOLLOWER, NOT A LEADER. NOW THAT YOU ARE CHIEF OF THE ZULU, HE WILL SEEK YOUR FAVOR.
THAT IS GOOD NEWS... BUT IT IS STILL NOT ENOUGH. WE NEED MORE TROOPS IF WE ARE TO DEFEAT ZWIDE.
DINGISWAYO HAS BECOME CARELESS, FOCUSING ONLY ON THE NEXT MAIDEN HE BEDS AND NEGLECTING THE AFFAIRS OF STATE.

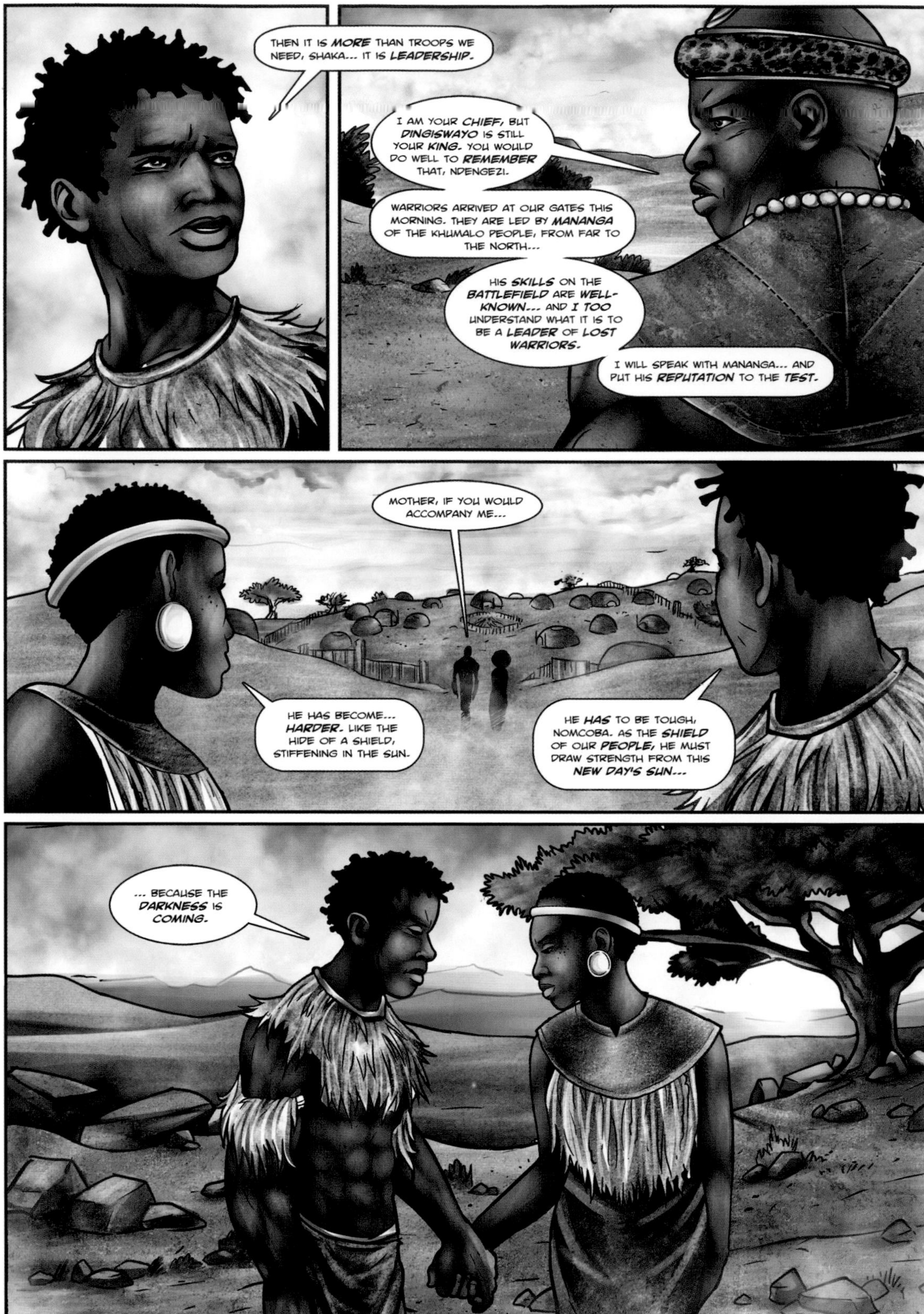
THEN IT IS MORE THAN TROOPS WE NEED, SHAKA... IT IS LEADERSHIP.
I AM YOUR CHIEF, BUT DINGISWAYO IS STILL YOUR KING. YOU WOULD DO WELL TO REMEMBER THAT, NDENGEZI.
WARRIORS ARRIVED AT OUR GATES THIS MORNING. THEY ARE LED BY MANANGA OF THE KHUMALO PEOPLE, FROM FAR TO THE NORTH...
HIS SKILLS ON THE BATTLEFIELD ARE WELL-KNOWN... AND I TOO UNDERSTAND WHAT IT IS TO BE A LEADER OF LOST WARRIORS.
I WILL SPEAK WITH MANANGA... AND PUT HIS REPUTATION TO THE TEST.
MOTHER, IF YOU WOULD ACCOMPANY ME...
HE HAS BECOME... HARDER. LIKE THE HIDE OF A SHIELD, STIFFENING IN THE SUN.
HE HAS TO BE TOUGH, NOMCOBA. AS THE SHIELD OF OUR PEOPLE, HE MUST DRAW STRENGTH FROM THIS NEW DAY'S SUN...
... BECAUSE THE DARKNESS IS COMING.

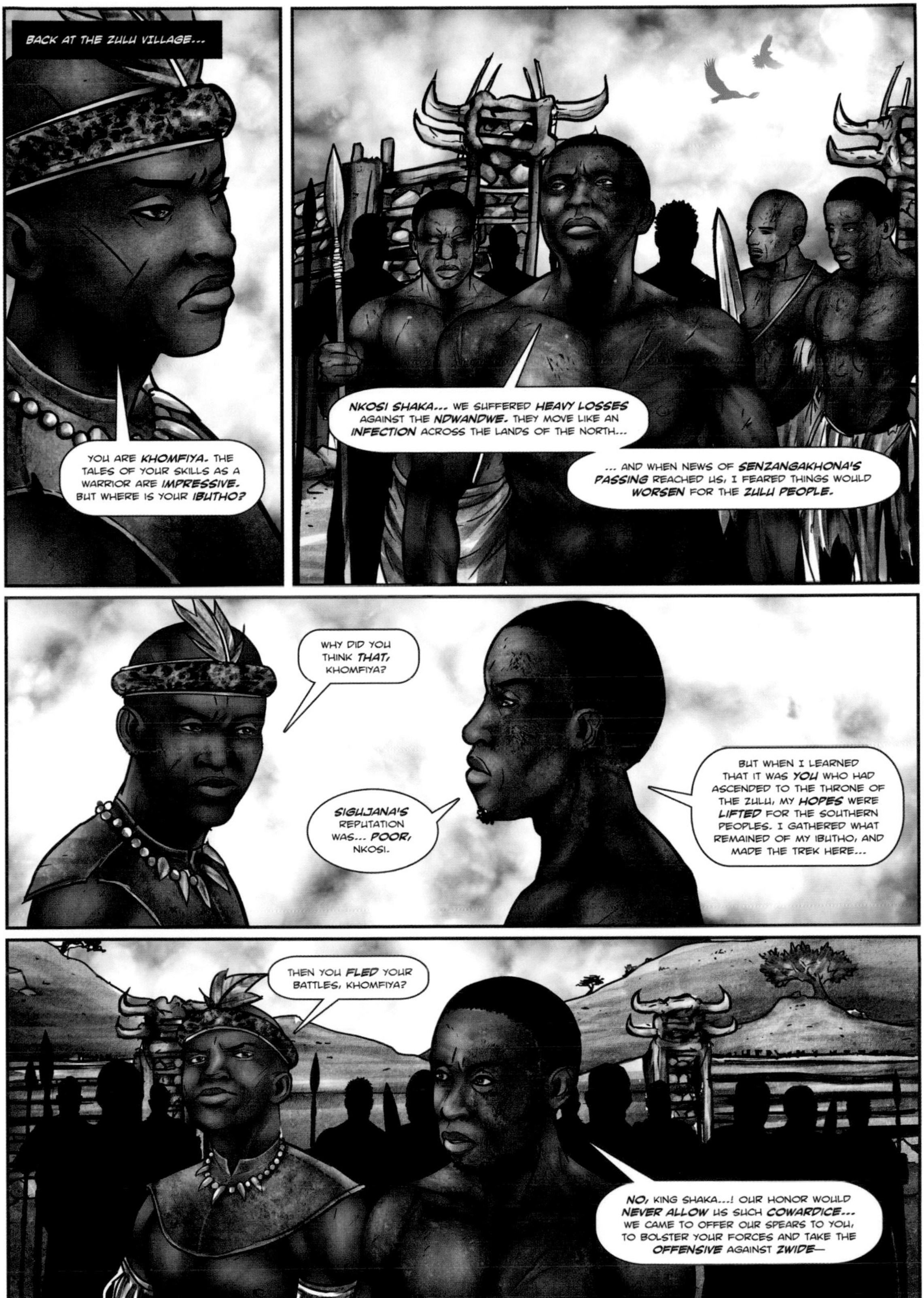
BACK AT THE ZULU VILLAGE...
YOU ARE KHOMFIYA. THE TALES OF YOUR SKILLS AS A WARRIOR ARE IMPRESSIVE. BUT WHERE IS YOUR IBUTHO?
NKOSI SHAKA... WE SUFFERED HEAVY LOSSES AGAINST THE NDWANDWE. THEY MOVE LIKE AN INFECTION ACROSS THE LANDS OF THE NORTH...
... AND WHEN NEWS OF SENZANGAKHONA'S PASSING REACHED US, I FEARED THINGS WOULD WORSEN FOR THE ZULU PEOPLE.
WHY DID YOU THINK THAT, KHOMFIYA?
SIGUJANA'S REPUTATION WAS... POOR, NKOSI.
BUT WHEN I LEARNED THAT IT WAS YOU WHO HAD ASCENDED TO THE THRONE OF THE ZULU, MY HOPES WERE LIFTED FOR THE SOUTHERN PEOPLES. I GATHERED WHAT REMAINED OF MY IBUTHO, AND MADE THE TREK HERE...
THEN YOU FLED YOUR BATTLES, KHOMFIYA?
NO, KING SHAKA...! OUR HONOR WOULD NEVER ALLOW US SUCH COWARDICE... WE CAME TO OFFER OUR SPEARS TO YOU, TO BOLSTER YOUR FORCES AND TAKE THE OFFENSIVE AGAINST ZWIDE—

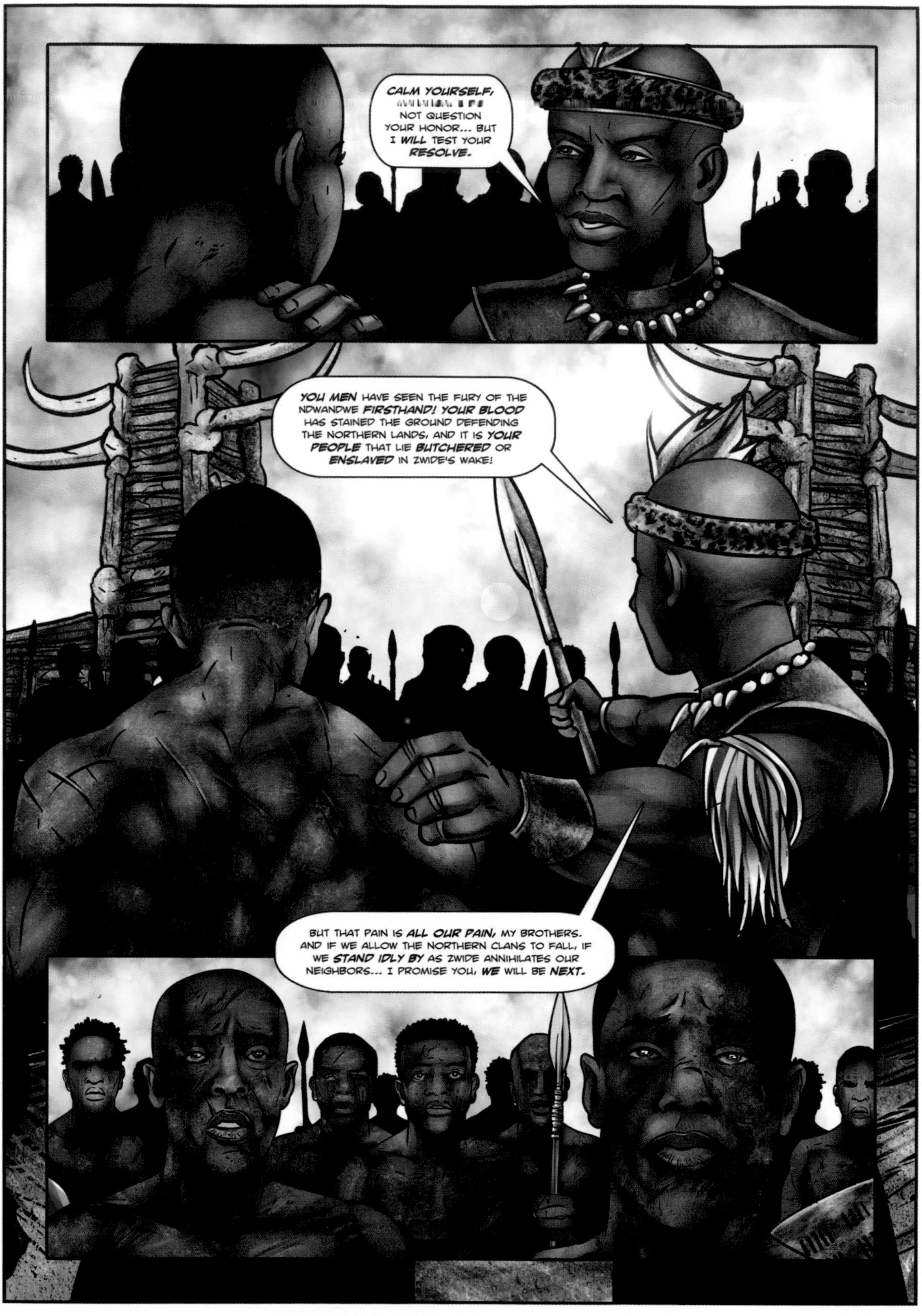

CALM YOURSELF, [redacted] NOT QUESTION YOUR HONOR... BUT I WILL TEST YOUR RESOLVE.
YOU MEN HAVE SEEN THE FURY OF THE NDWANDWE FIRSTHAND! YOUR BLOOD HAS STAINED THE GROUND DEFENDING THE NORTHERN LANDS, AND IT IS YOUR PEOPLE THAT LIE BUTCHERED OR ENSLAVED IN ZWIDE'S WAKE!
BUT THAT PAIN IS ALL OUR PAIN, MY BROTHERS. AND IF WE ALLOW THE NORTHERN CLANS TO FALL, IF WE STAND IDLY BY AS ZWIDE ANNIHILATES OUR NEIGHBORS... I PROMISE YOU, WE WILL BE NEXT.

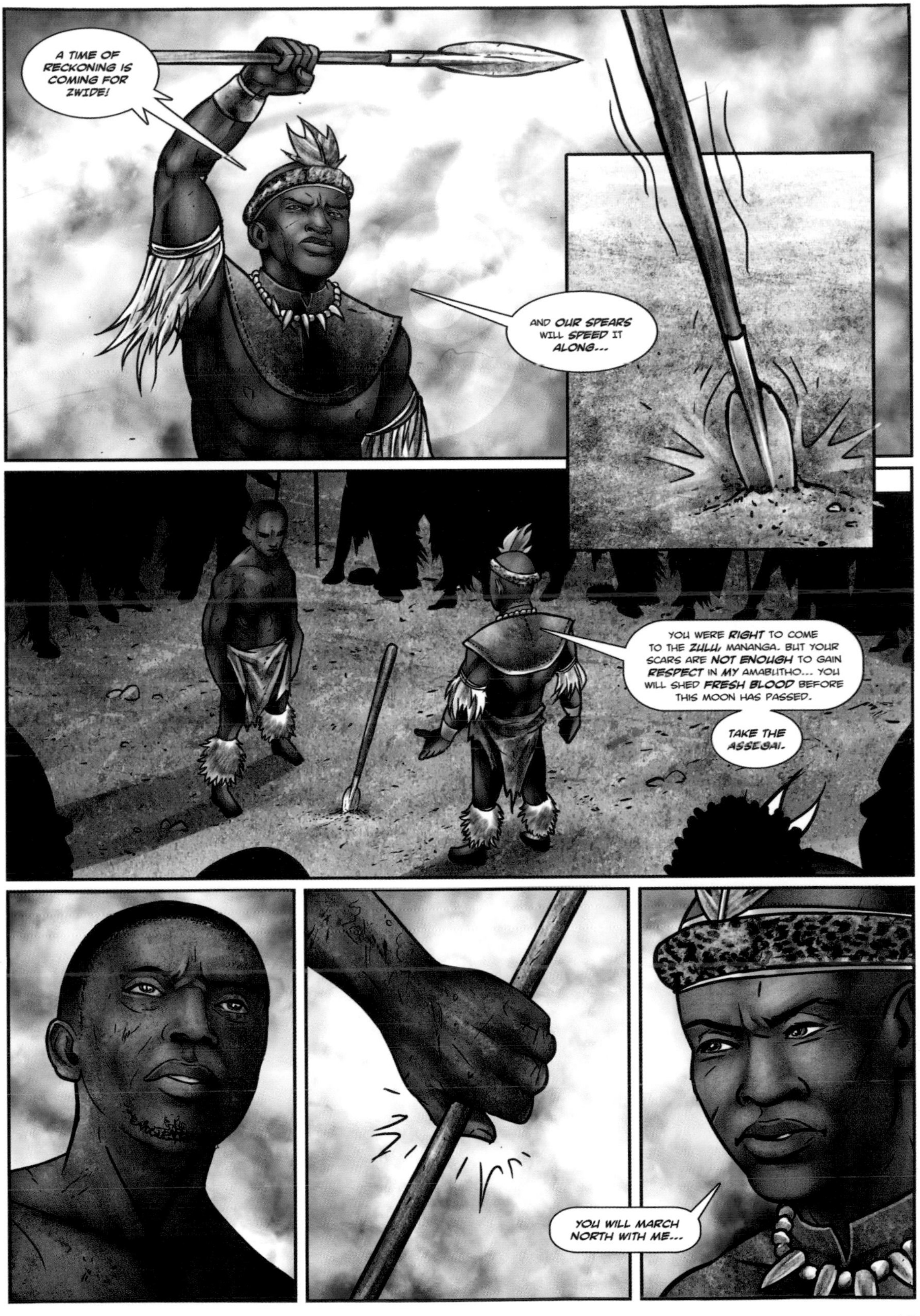

A TIME OF RECKONING IS COMING FOR ZWIDE!
AND OUR SPEARS WILL SPEED IT ALONG...
YOU WERE RIGHT TO COME TO THE ZULU, MANANGA. BUT YOUR SCARS ARE NOT ENOUGH TO GAIN RESPECT IN MY AMABUTHO... YOU WILL SHED FRESH BLOOD BEFORE THIS MOON HAS PASSED.
TAKE THE ASSEGAI.
YOU WILL MARCH NORTH WITH ME...

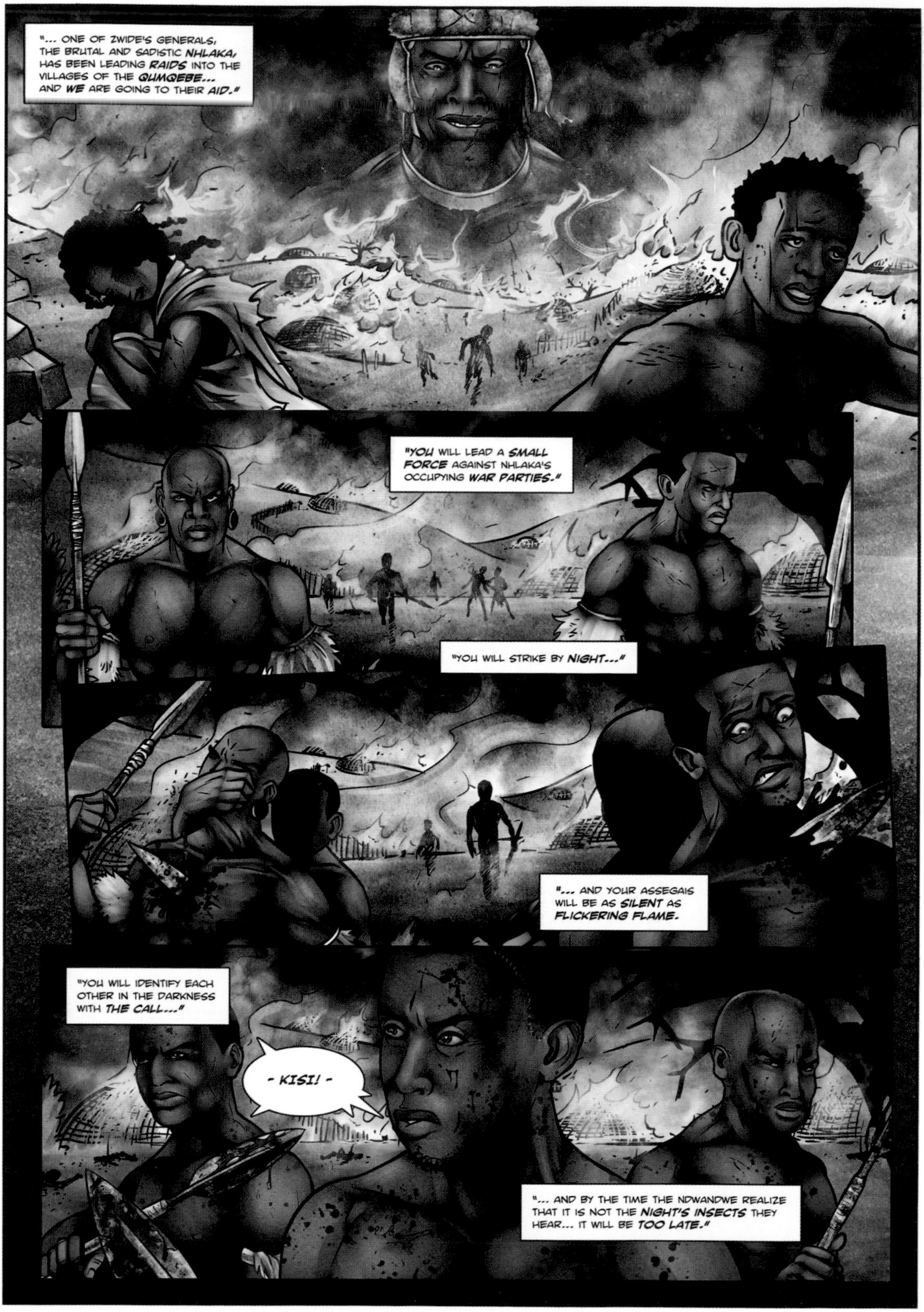
"... ONE OF ZWIDE'S GENERALS, THE BRUTAL AND SADISTIC NHLAKA, HAS BEEN LEADING RAIDS INTO THE VILLAGES OF THE QUMQEBE... AND WE ARE GOING TO THEIR AID."
"YOU WILL LEAD A SMALL FORCE AGAINST NHLAKA'S OCCUPYING WAR PARTIES."
"YOU WILL STRIKE BY NIGHT..."
"... AND YOUR ASSEGAIS WILL BE AS SILENT AS FLICKERING FLAME.
"YOU WILL IDENTIFY EACH OTHER IN THE DARKNESS WITH THE CALL..."
- KISI! -
"... AND BY THE TIME THE NDWANDWE REALIZE THAT IT IS NOT THE NIGHT'S INSECTS THEY HEAR... IT WILL BE TOO LATE."

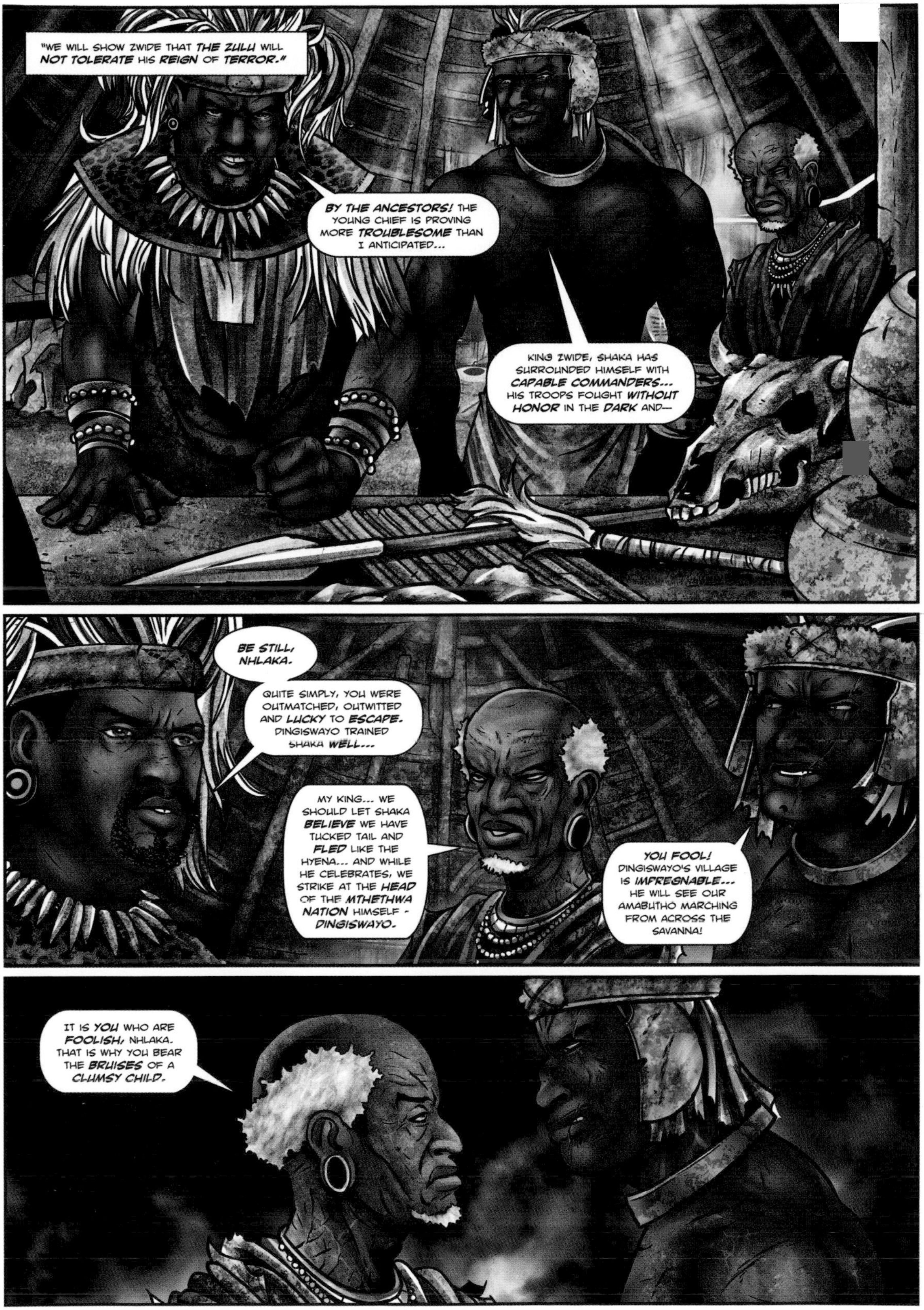
"WE WILL SHOW ZWIDE THAT THE ZULU WILL NOT TOLERATE HIS REIGN OF TERROR."
BY THE ANCESTORS! THE YOUNG CHIEF IS PROVING MORE TROUBLESOME THAN I ANTICIPATED...
KING ZWIDE, SHAKA HAS SURROUNDED HIMSELF WITH CAPABLE COMMANDERS... HIS TROOPS FOUGHT WITHOUT HONOR IN THE DARK AND—
BE STILL, NHLAKA.
QUITE SIMPLY, YOU WERE OUTMATCHED, OUTWITTED AND LUCKY TO ESCAPE. DINGISWAYO TRAINED SHAKA WELL...
MY KING... WE SHOULD LET SHAKA BELIEVE WE HAVE TUCKED TAIL AND FLED LIKE THE HYENA... AND WHILE HE CELEBRATES, WE STRIKE AT THE HEAD OF THE MTHETHWA NATION HIMSELF - DINGISWAYO.
YOU FOOL! DINGISWAYO'S VILLAGE IS IMPREGNABLE... HE WILL SEE OUR AMABUTHO MARCHING FROM ACROSS THE SAVANNA!
IT IS YOU WHO ARE FOOLISH, NHLAKA. THAT IS WHY YOU BEAR THE BRUISES OF A CLUMSY CHILD.

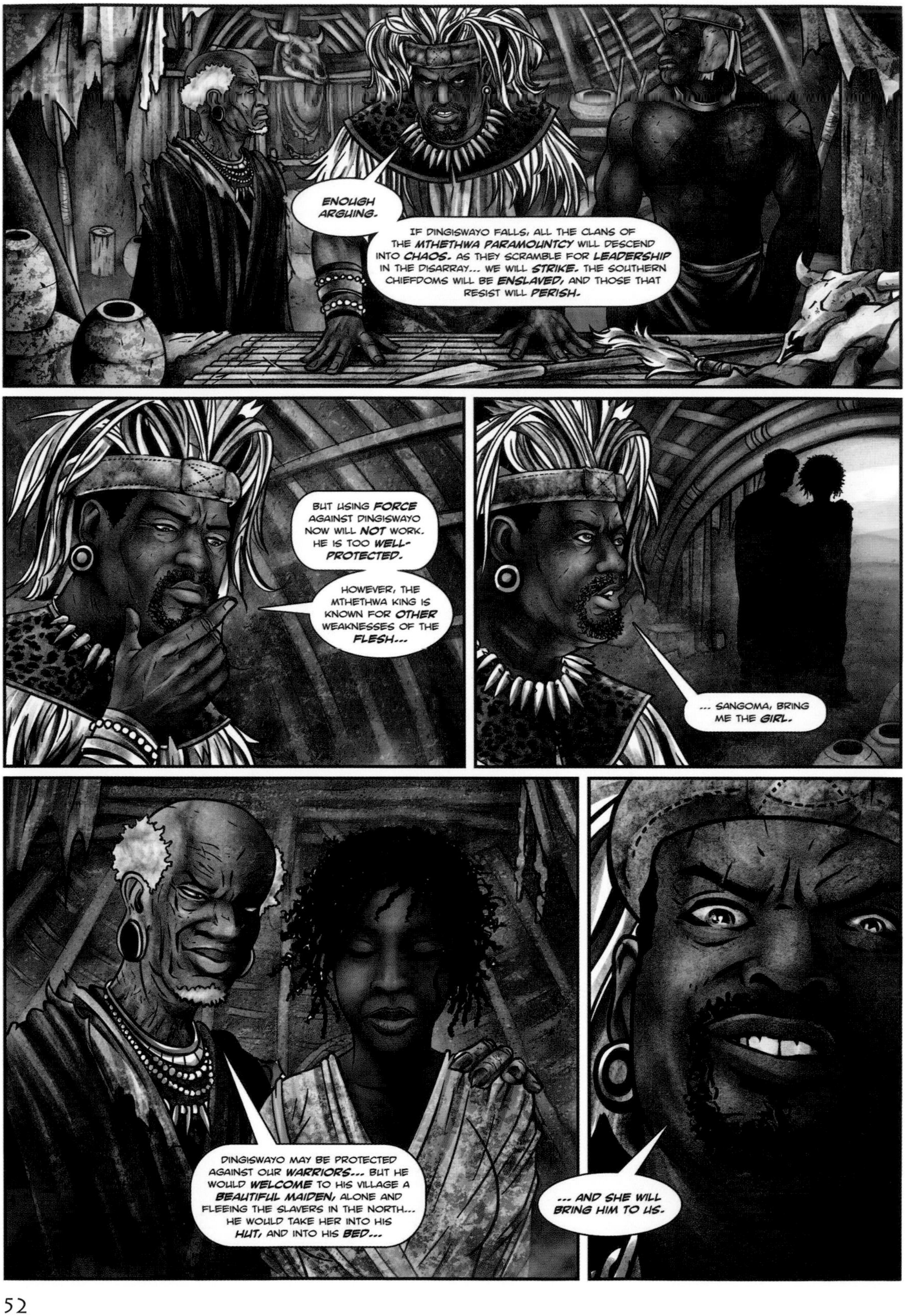

ENOUGH ARGUING.
IF DINGISWAYO FALLS, ALL THE CLANS OF THE MTHETHWA PARAMOUNTCY WILL DESCEND INTO CHAOS. AS THEY SCRAMBLE FOR LEADERSHIP IN THE DISARRAY... WE WILL STRIKE. THE SOUTHERN CHIEFDOMS WILL BE ENSLAVED, AND THOSE THAT RESIST WILL PERISH.
BUT USING FORCE AGAINST DINGISWAYO NOW WILL NOT WORK. HE IS TOO WELL-PROTECTED.
HOWEVER, THE MTHETHWA KING IS KNOWN FOR OTHER WEAKNESSES OF THE FLESH...
... SANGOMA, BRING ME THE GIRL.
DINGISWAYO MAY BE PROTECTED AGAINST OUR WARRIORS... BUT HE WOULD WELCOME TO HIS VILLAGE A BEAUTIFUL MAIDEN, ALONE AND FLEEING THE SLAVERS IN THE NORTH... HE WOULD TAKE HER INTO HIS HUT, AND INTO HIS BED...
... AND SHE WILL BRING HIM TO US.

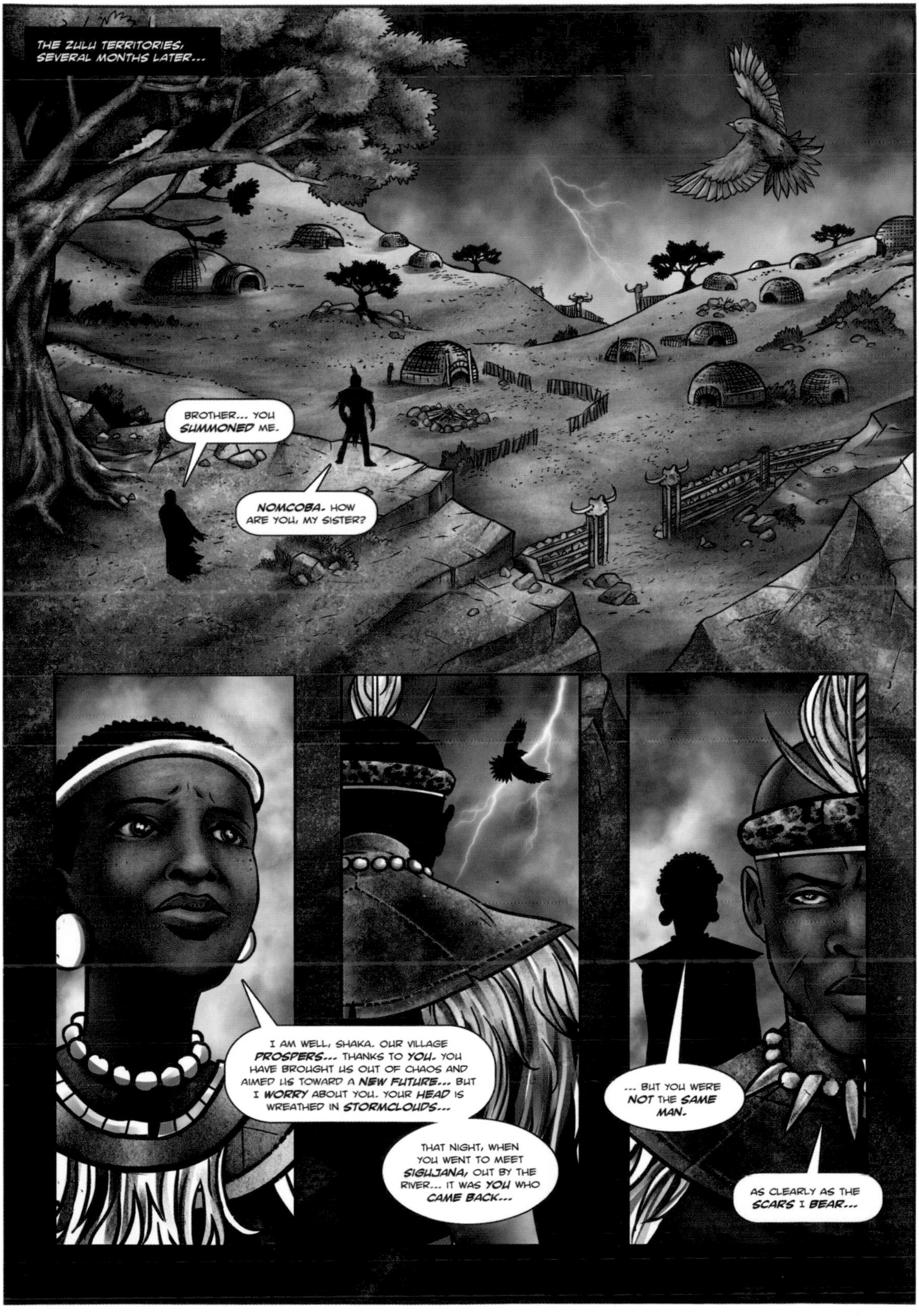
THE ZULU TERRITORIES, SEVERAL MONTHS LATER...
BROTHER... YOU SUMMONED ME.
NOMCOBA. HOW ARE YOU, MY SISTER?
I AM WELL, SHAKA. OUR VILLAGE PROSPERS... THANKS TO YOU. YOU HAVE BROUGHT US OUT OF CHAOS AND AIMED US TOWARD A NEW FUTURE... BUT I WORRY ABOUT YOU. YOUR HEAD IS WREATHED IN STORMCLOUDS...
THAT NIGHT, WHEN YOU WENT TO MEET SIGUJANA, OUT BY THE RIVER... IT WAS YOU WHO CAME BACK...
... BUT YOU WERE NOT THE SAME MAN.
AS CLEARLY AS THE SCARS I BEAR...

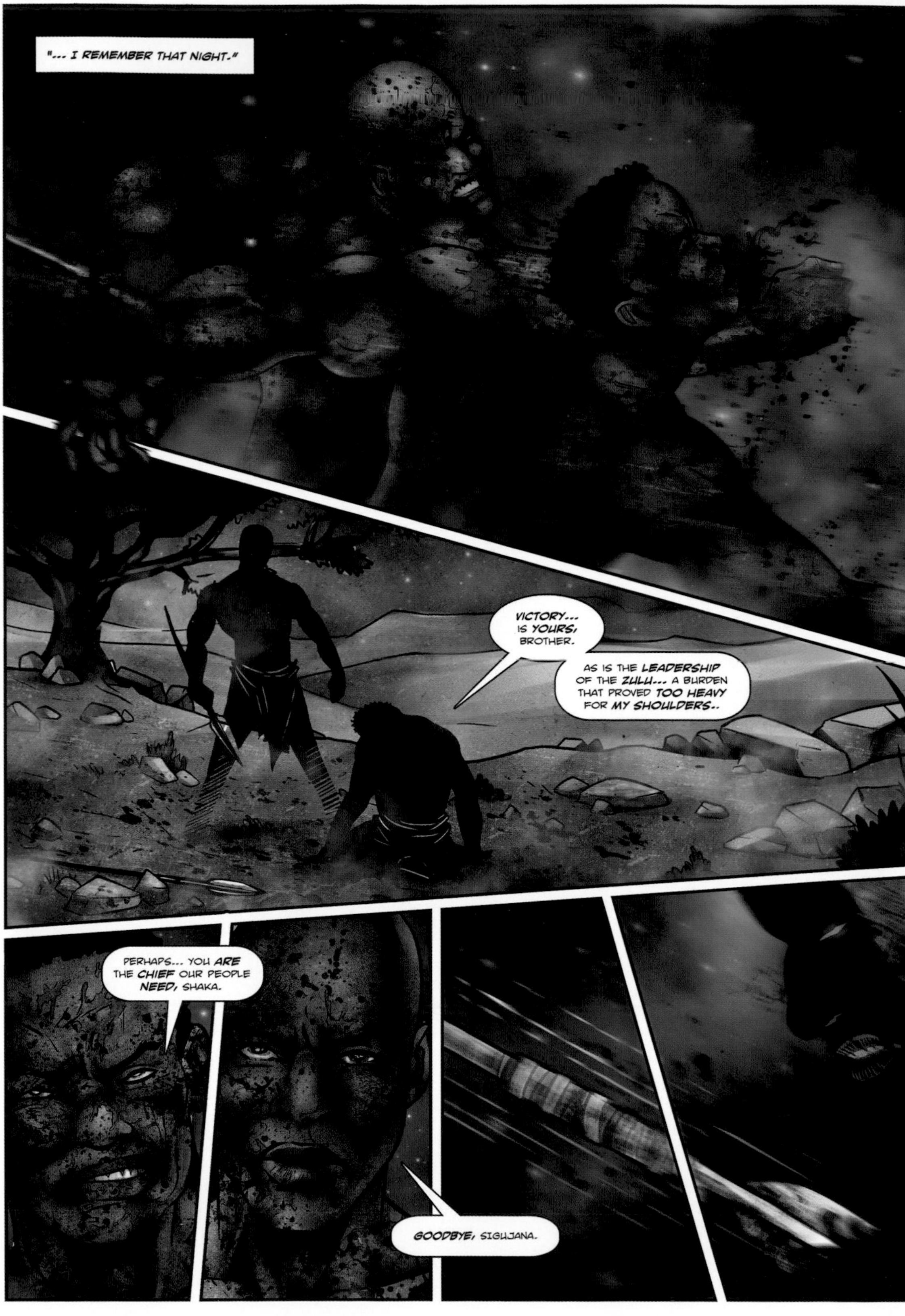
"... I REMEMBER THAT NIGHT."
VICTORY... IS YOURS, BROTHER.
AS IS THE LEADERSHIP OF THE ZULU... A BURDEN THAT PROVED TOO HEAVY FOR MY SHOULDERS..
PERHAPS... YOU ARE THE CHIEF OUR PEOPLE NEED, SHAKA.
GOODBYE, SIGUJANA.

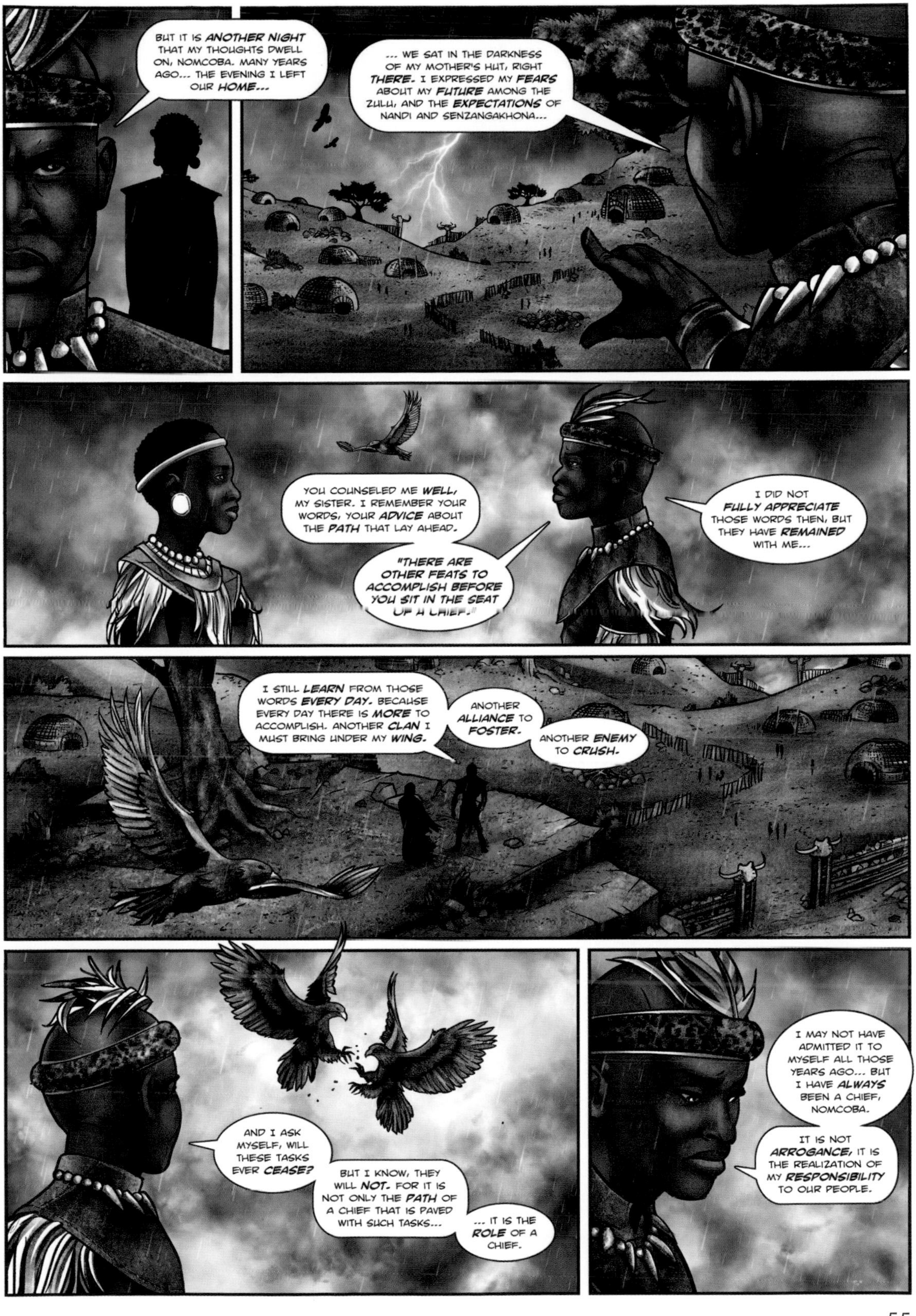
BUT IT IS ANOTHER NIGHT THAT MY THOUGHTS DWELL ON, NOMCOBA. MANY YEARS AGO... THE EVENING I LEFT OUR HOME...
... WE SAT IN THE DARKNESS OF MY MOTHER'S HUT, RIGHT THERE. I EXPRESSED MY FEARS ABOUT MY FUTURE AMONG THE ZULU, AND THE EXPECTATIONS OF NANDI AND SENZANGAKHONA...
YOU COUNSELED ME WELL, MY SISTER. I REMEMBER YOUR WORDS, YOUR ADVICE ABOUT THE PATH THAT LAY AHEAD.
"THERE ARE OTHER FEATS TO ACCOMPLISH BEFORE YOU SIT IN THE SEAT OF A CHIEF."
I DID NOT FULLY APPRECIATE THOSE WORDS THEN, BUT THEY HAVE REMAINED WITH ME...
I STILL LEARN FROM THOSE WORDS EVERY DAY. BECAUSE EVERY DAY THERE IS MORE TO ACCOMPLISH. ANOTHER CLAN I MUST BRING UNDER MY WING.
ANOTHER ALLIANCE TO FOSTER.
ANOTHER ENEMY TO CRUSH.
AND I ASK MYSELF, WILL THESE TASKS EVER CEASE?
BUT I KNOW, THEY WILL NOT. FOR IT IS NOT ONLY THE PATH OF A CHIEF THAT IS PAVED WITH SUCH TASKS...
... IT IS THE ROLE OF A CHIEF.
I MAY NOT HAVE ADMITTED IT TO MYSELF ALL THOSE YEARS AGO... BUT I HAVE ALWAYS BEEN A CHIEF, NOMCOBA.
IT IS NOT ARROGANCE, IT IS THE REALIZATION OF MY RESPONSIBILITY TO OUR PEOPLE.

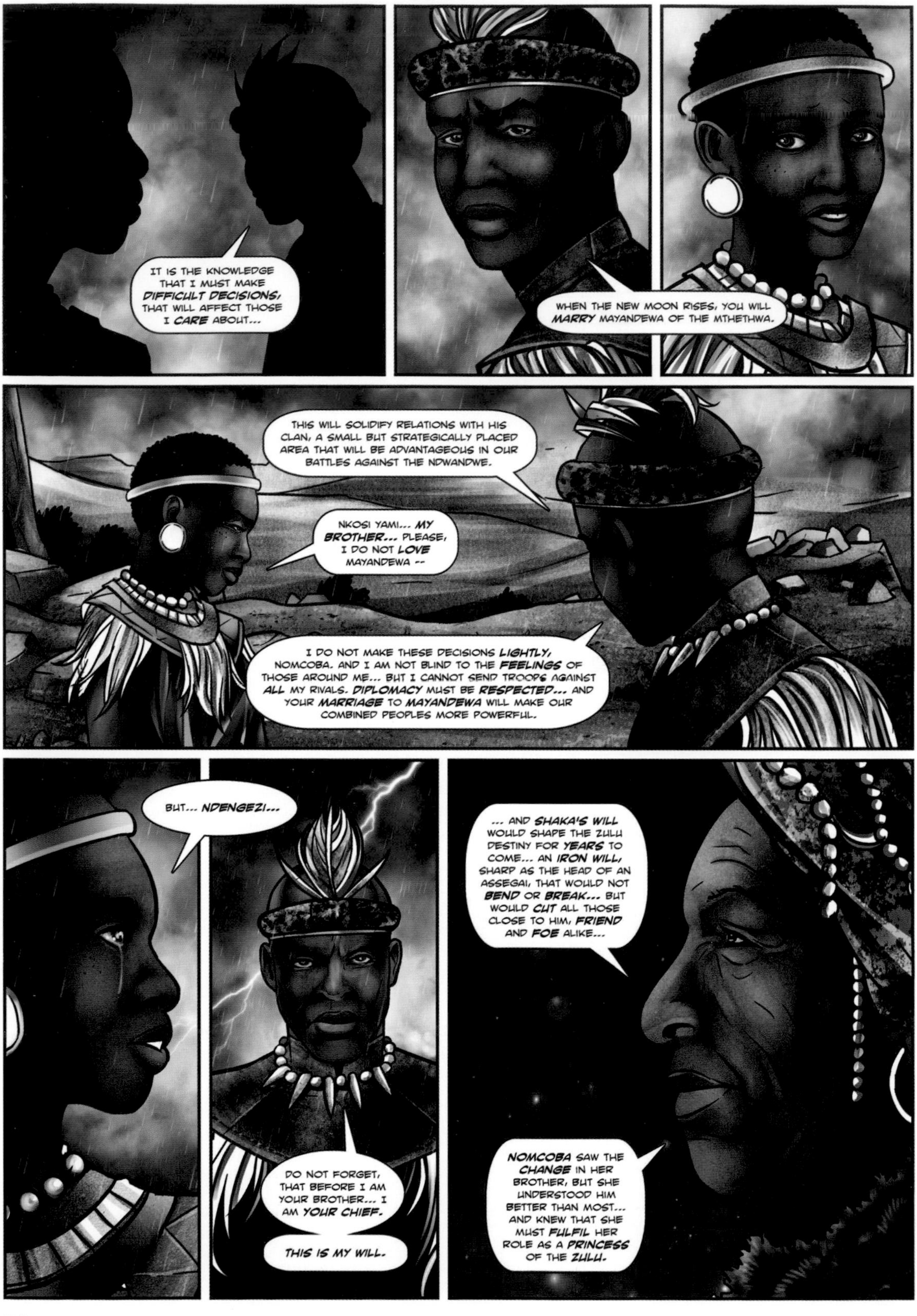
IT IS THE KNOWLEDGE THAT I MUST MAKE DIFFICULT DECISIONS, THAT WILL AFFECT THOSE I CARE ABOUT...
WHEN THE NEW MOON RISES, YOU WILL MARRY MAYANDEWA OF THE MTHETHWA.
THIS WILL SOLIDIFY RELATIONS WITH HIS CLAN, A SMALL BUT STRATEGICALLY PLACED AREA THAT WILL BE ADVANTAGEOUS IN OUR BATTLES AGAINST THE NDWANDWE.
NKOSI YAMI... MY BROTHER... PLEASE, I DO NOT LOVE MAYANDEWA --
I DO NOT MAKE THESE DECISIONS LIGHTLY, NOMCOBA. AND I AM NOT BLIND TO THE FEELINGS OF THOSE AROUND ME... BUT I CANNOT SEND TROOPS AGAINST ALL MY RIVALS. DIPLOMACY MUST BE RESPECTED... AND YOUR MARRIAGE TO MAYANDEWA WILL MAKE OUR COMBINED PEOPLES MORE POWERFUL.
BUT... NDENGEZI...
DO NOT FORGET, THAT BEFORE I AM YOUR BROTHER... I AM YOUR CHIEF.
THIS IS MY WILL.
... AND SHAKA'S WILL WOULD SHAPE THE ZULU DESTINY FOR YEARS TO COME... AN IRON WILL, SHARP AS THE HEAD OF AN ASSEGAI, THAT WOULD NOT BEND OR BREAK... BUT WOULD CUT ALL THOSE CLOSE TO HIM, FRIEND AND FOE ALIKE...
NOMCOBA SAW THE CHANGE IN HER BROTHER, BUT SHE UNDERSTOOD HIM BETTER THAN MOST... AND KNEW THAT SHE MUST FULFIL HER ROLE AS A PRINCESS OF THE ZULU.

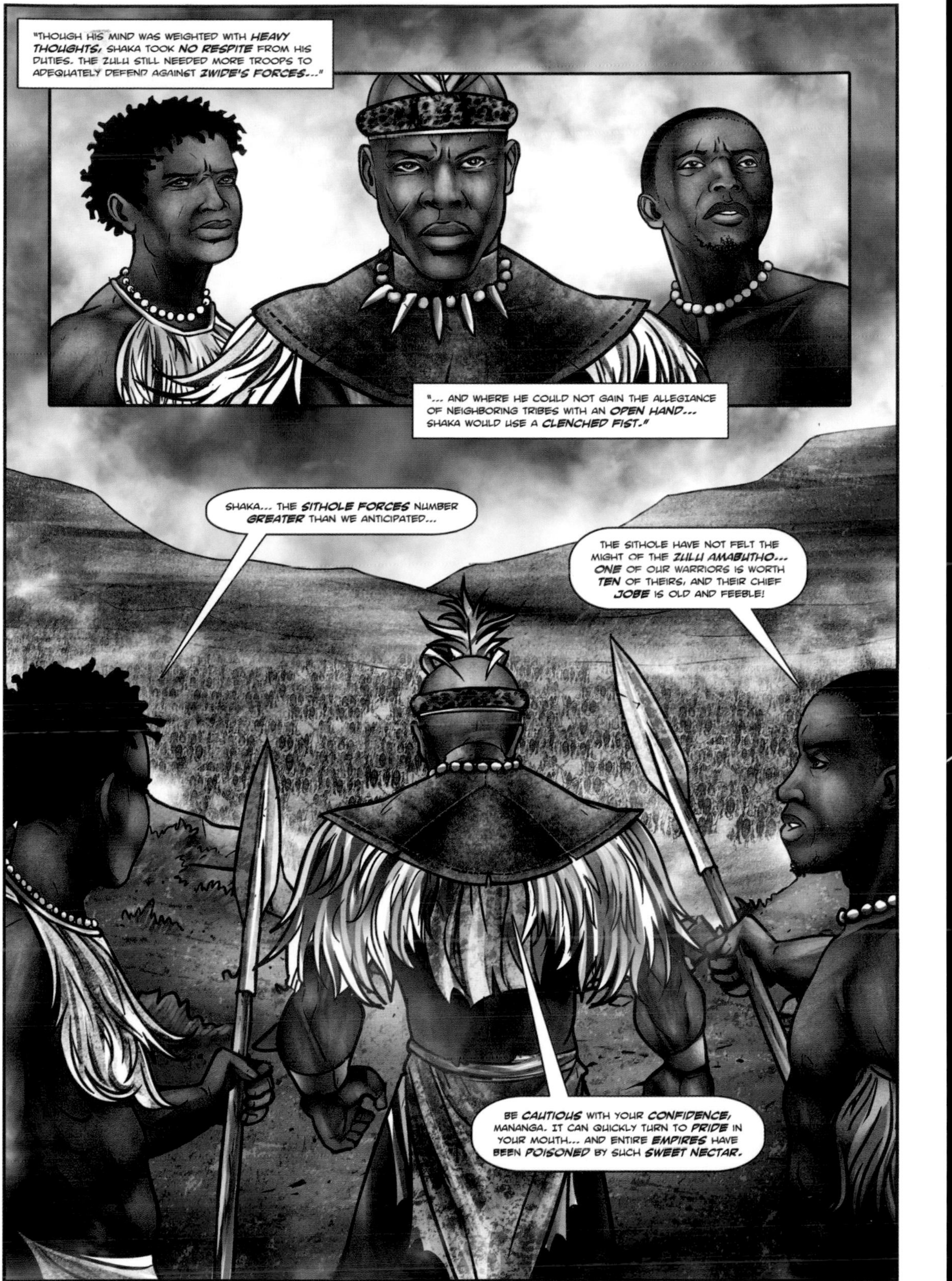
"THOUGH HIS MIND WAS WEIGHTED WITH HEAVY THOUGHTS, SHAKA TOOK NO RESPITE FROM HIS DUTIES. THE ZULU STILL NEEDED MORE TROOPS TO ADEQUATELY DEFEND AGAINST ZWIDE'S FORCES..."
"... AND WHERE HE COULD NOT GAIN THE ALLEGIANCE OF NEIGHBORING TRIBES WITH AN OPEN HAND... SHAKA WOULD USE A CLENCHED FIST."
SHAKA... THE SITHOLE FORCES NUMBER GREATER THAN WE ANTICIPATED...
THE SITHOLE HAVE NOT FELT THE MIGHT OF THE ZULU AMABUTHO... ONE OF OUR WARRIORS IS WORTH TEN OF THEIRS, AND THEIR CHIEF JOBE IS OLD AND FEEBLE!
BE CAUTIOUS WITH YOUR CONFIDENCE, MANANGA. IT CAN QUICKLY TURN TO PRIDE IN YOUR MOUTH... AND ENTIRE EMPIRES HAVE BEEN POISONED BY SUCH SWEET NECTAR.

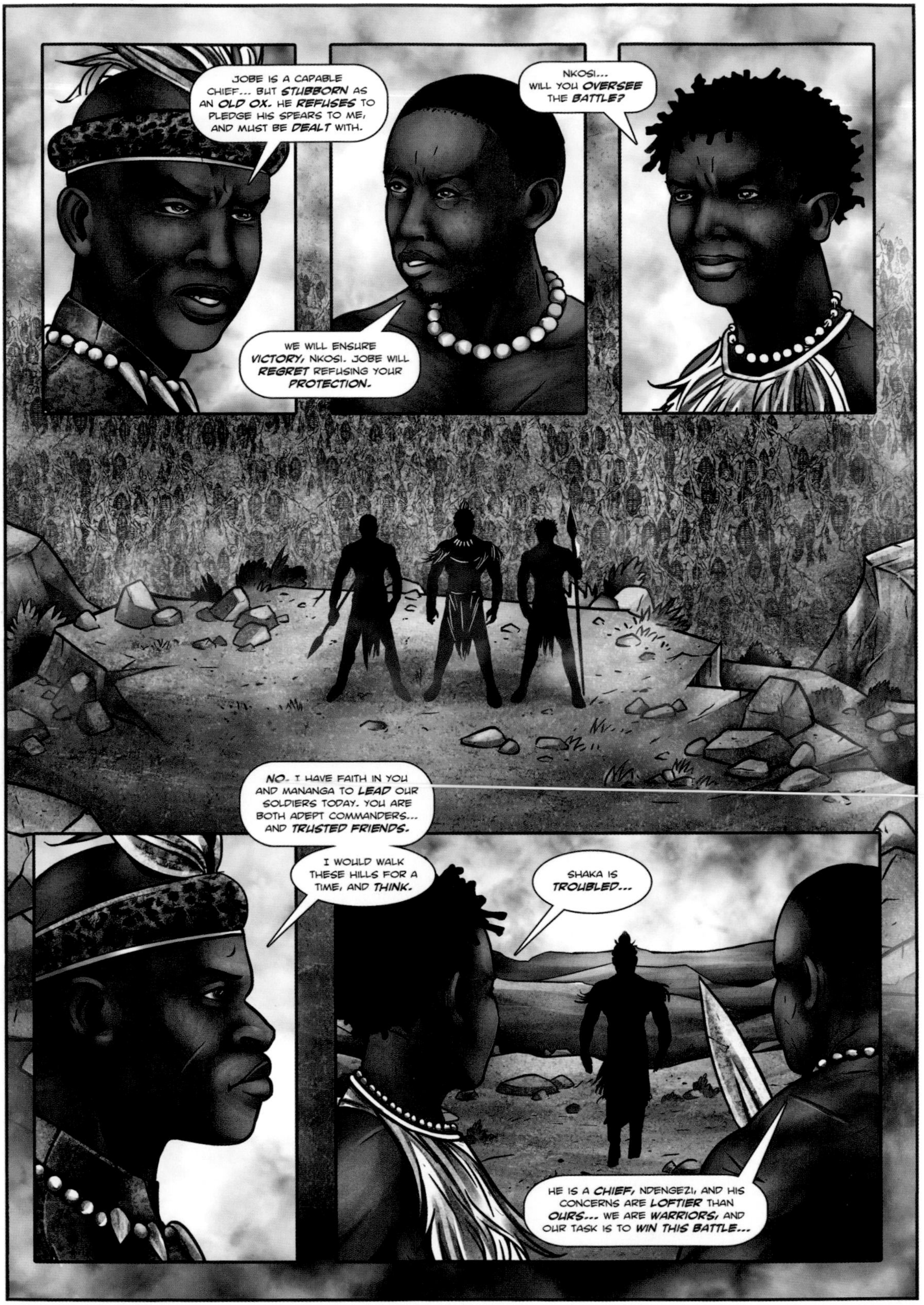
JOBE IS A CAPABLE CHIEF... BUT STUBBORN AS AN OLD OX. HE REFUSES TO PLEDGE HIS SPEARS TO ME, AND MUST BE DEALT WITH.
WE WILL ENSURE VICTORY, NKOSI. JOBE WILL REGRET REFUSING YOUR PROTECTION.
NKOSI... WILL YOU OVERSEE THE BATTLE?
NO. I HAVE FAITH IN YOU AND MANANGA TO LEAD OUR SOLDIERS TODAY. YOU ARE BOTH ADEPT COMMANDERS... AND TRUSTED FRIENDS.
I WOULD WALK THESE HILLS FOR A TIME, AND THINK.
SHAKA IS TROUBLED...
HE IS A CHIEF, NDENGEZI, AND HIS CONCERNS ARE LOFTIER THAN OURS... WE ARE WARRIORS, AND OUR TASK IS TO WIN THIS BATTLE...

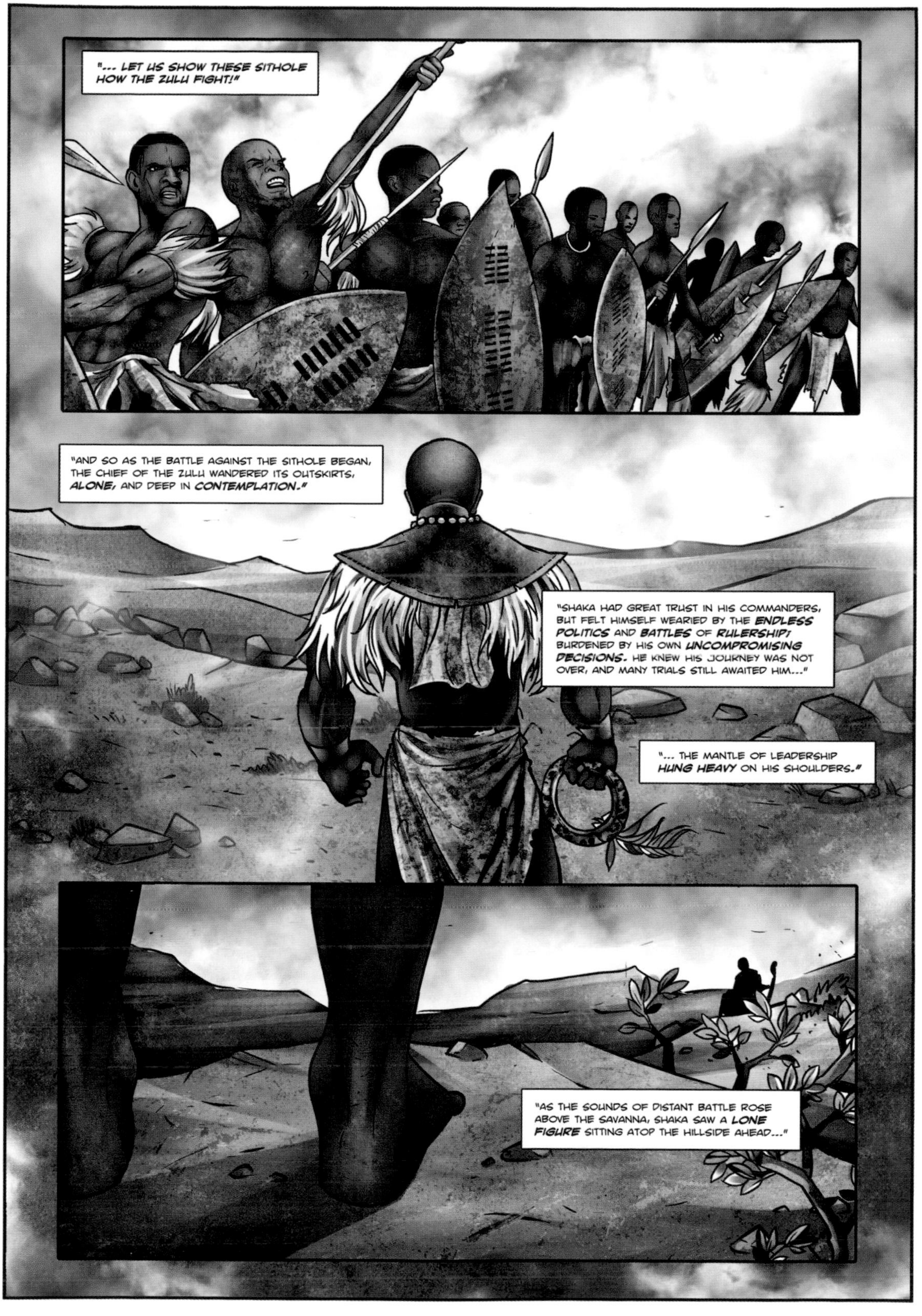
"... LET US SHOW THESE SITHOLE HOW THE ZULU FIGHT!"
"AND SO AS THE BATTLE AGAINST THE SITHOLE BEGAN, THE CHIEF OF THE ZULU WANDERED ITS OUTSKIRTS, ALONE, AND DEEP IN CONTEMPLATION."
"SHAKA HAD GREAT TRUST IN HIS COMMANDERS, BUT FELT HIMSELF WEARIED BY THE ENDLESS POLITICS AND BATTLES OF RULERSHIP; BURDENED BY HIS OWN UNCOMPROMISING DECISIONS. HE KNEW HIS JOURNEY WAS NOT OVER, AND MANY TRIALS STILL AWAITED HIM..."
"... THE MANTLE OF LEADERSHIP HUNG HEAVY ON HIS SHOULDERS."
"AS THE SOUNDS OF DISTANT BATTLE ROSE ABOVE THE SAVANNA, SHAKA SAW A LONE FIGURE SITTING ATOP THE HILLSIDE AHEAD..."

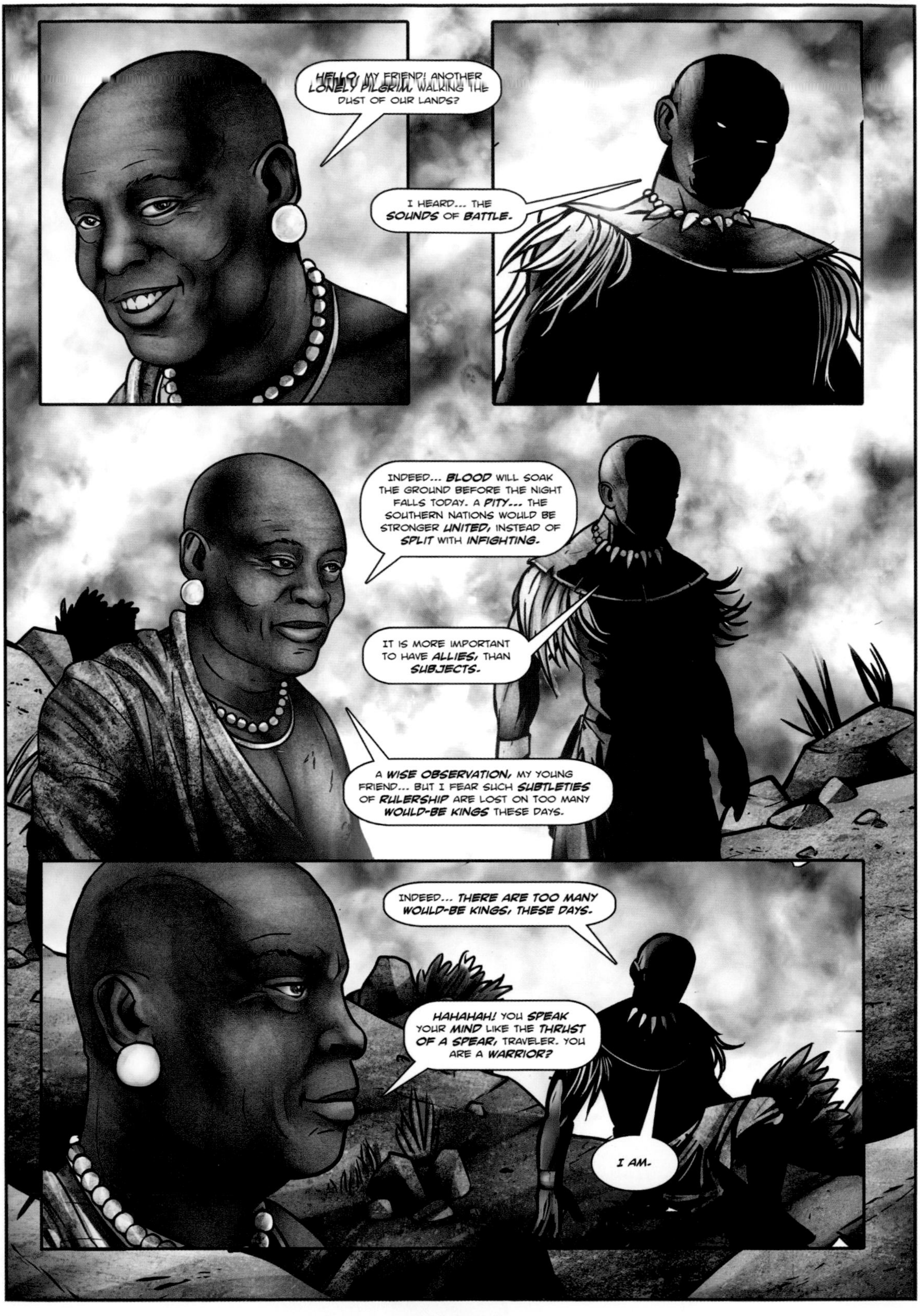
HELLO, MY FRIEND! ANOTHER LONELY PILGRIM, WALKING THE DUST OF OUR LANDS?
I HEARD... THE SOUNDS OF BATTLE.
INDEED... BLOOD WILL SOAK THE GROUND BEFORE THE NIGHT FALLS TODAY. A PITY... THE SOUTHERN NATIONS WOULD BE STRONGER UNITED, INSTEAD OF SPLIT WITH INFIGHTING.
IT IS MORE IMPORTANT TO HAVE ALLIES, THAN SUBJECTS.
A WISE OBSERVATION, MY YOUNG FRIEND... BUT I FEAR SUCH SUBTLETIES OF RULERSHIP ARE LOST ON TOO MANY WOULD-BE KINGS THESE DAYS.
INDEED... THERE ARE TOO MANY WOULD-BE KINGS, THESE DAYS.
HAHAHAH! YOU SPEAK YOUR MIND LIKE THE THRUST OF A SPEAR, TRAVELER. YOU ARE A WARRIOR?
I AM.

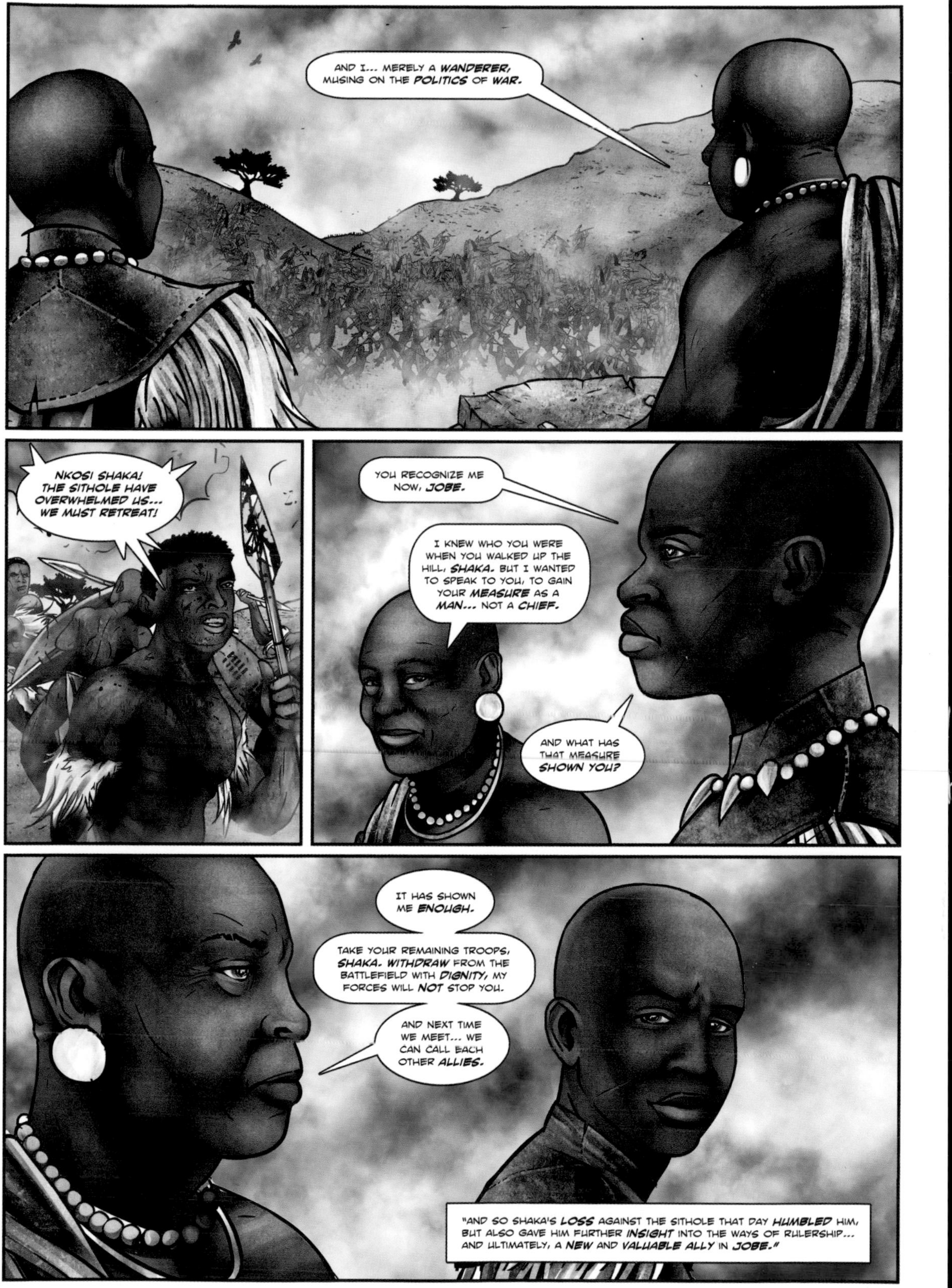
AND I... MERELY A WANDERER, MUSING ON THE POLITICS OF WAR.
NKOSI SHAKA! THE SITHOLE HAVE OVERWHELMED US... WE MUST RETREAT!
YOU RECOGNIZE ME NOW, JOBE.
I KNEW WHO YOU WERE WHEN YOU WALKED UP THE HILL, SHAKA. BUT I WANTED TO SPEAK TO YOU, TO GAIN YOUR MEASURE AS A MAN... NOT A CHIEF.
AND WHAT HAS THAT MEASURE SHOWN YOU?
IT HAS SHOWN ME ENOUGH.
TAKE YOUR REMAINING TROOPS, SHAKA. WITHDRAW FROM THE BATTLEFIELD WITH DIGNITY, MY FORCES WILL NOT STOP YOU.
AND NEXT TIME WE MEET... WE CAN CALL EACH OTHER ALLIES.
"AND SO SHAKA'S LOSS AGAINST THE SITHOLE THAT DAY HUMBLED HIM, BUT ALSO GAVE HIM FURTHER INSIGHT INTO THE WAYS OF RULERSHIP... AND ULTIMATELY, A NEW AND VALUABLE ALLY IN JOBE."

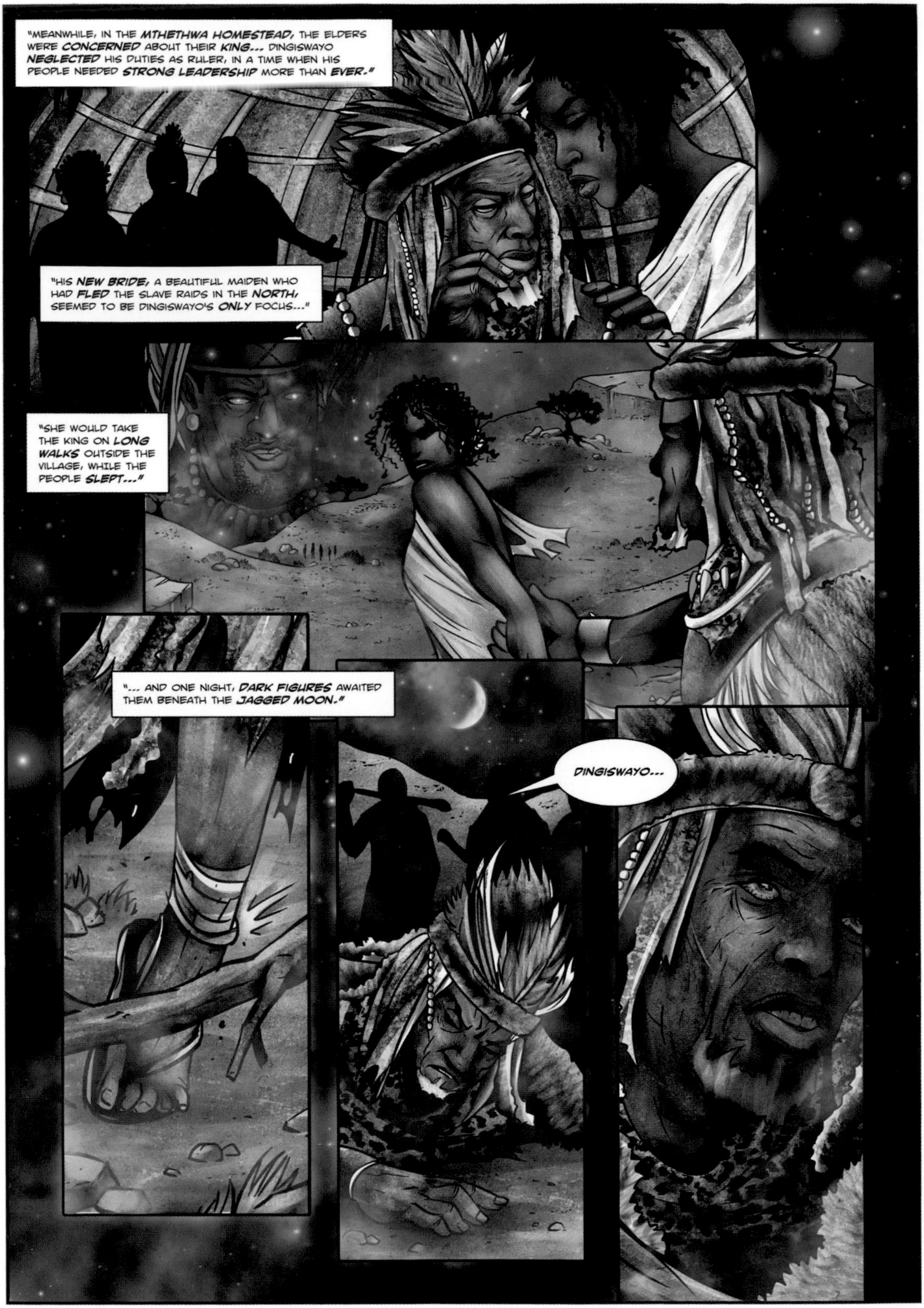
"MEANWHILE, IN THE MTHETHWA HOMESTEAD, THE ELDERS WERE CONCERNED ABOUT THEIR KING... DINGISWAYO NEGLECTED HIS DUTIES AS RULER, IN A TIME WHEN HIS PEOPLE NEEDED STRONG LEADERSHIP MORE THAN EVER."
"HIS NEW BRIDE, A BEAUTIFUL MAIDEN WHO HAD FLED THE SLAVE RAIDS IN THE NORTH, SEEMED TO BE DINGISWAYO'S ONLY FOCUS..."
"SHE WOULD TAKE THE KING ON LONG WALKS OUTSIDE THE VILLAGE, WHILE THE PEOPLE SLEPT..."
"... AND ONE NIGHT, DARK FIGURES AWAITED THEM BENEATH THE JAGGED MOON."
DINGISWAYO...

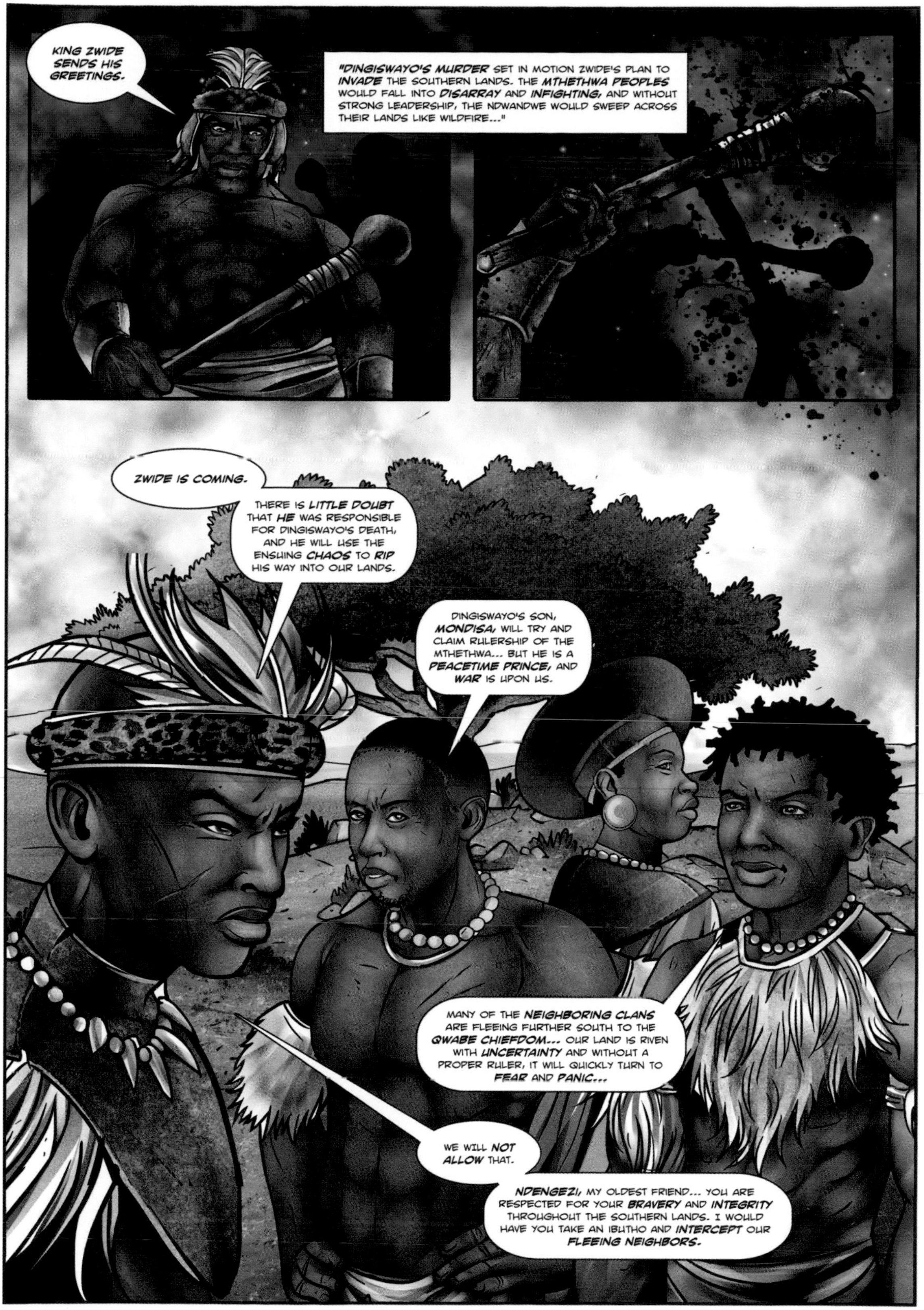
KING ZWIDE SENDS HIS GREETINGS.
"DINGISWAYO'S MURDER SET IN MOTION ZWIDE'S PLAN TO INVADE THE SOUTHERN LANDS. THE MTHETHWA PEOPLES WOULD FALL INTO DISARRAY AND INFIGHTING, AND WITHOUT STRONG LEADERSHIP, THE NDWANDWE WOULD SWEEP ACROSS THEIR LANDS LIKE WILDFIRE..."
ZWIDE IS COMING.
THERE IS LITTLE DOUBT THAT HE WAS RESPONSIBLE FOR DINGISWAYO'S DEATH, AND HE WILL USE THE ENSUING CHAOS TO RIP HIS WAY INTO OUR LANDS.
DINGISWAYO'S SON, MONDISA, WILL TRY AND CLAIM RULERSHIP OF THE MTHETHWA... BUT HE IS A PEACETIME PRINCE, AND WAR IS UPON US.
MANY OF THE NEIGHBORING CLANS ARE FLEEING FURTHER SOUTH TO THE QWABE CHIEFDOM... OUR LAND IS RIVEN WITH UNCERTAINTY AND WITHOUT A PROPER RULER, IT WILL QUICKLY TURN TO FEAR AND PANIC...
WE WILL NOT ALLOW THAT.
NDENGEZI, MY OLDEST FRIEND... YOU ARE RESPECTED FOR YOUR BRAVERY AND INTEGRITY THROUGHOUT THE SOUTHERN LANDS. I WOULD HAVE YOU TAKE AN IBUTHO AND INTERCEPT OUR FLEEING NEIGHBORS.

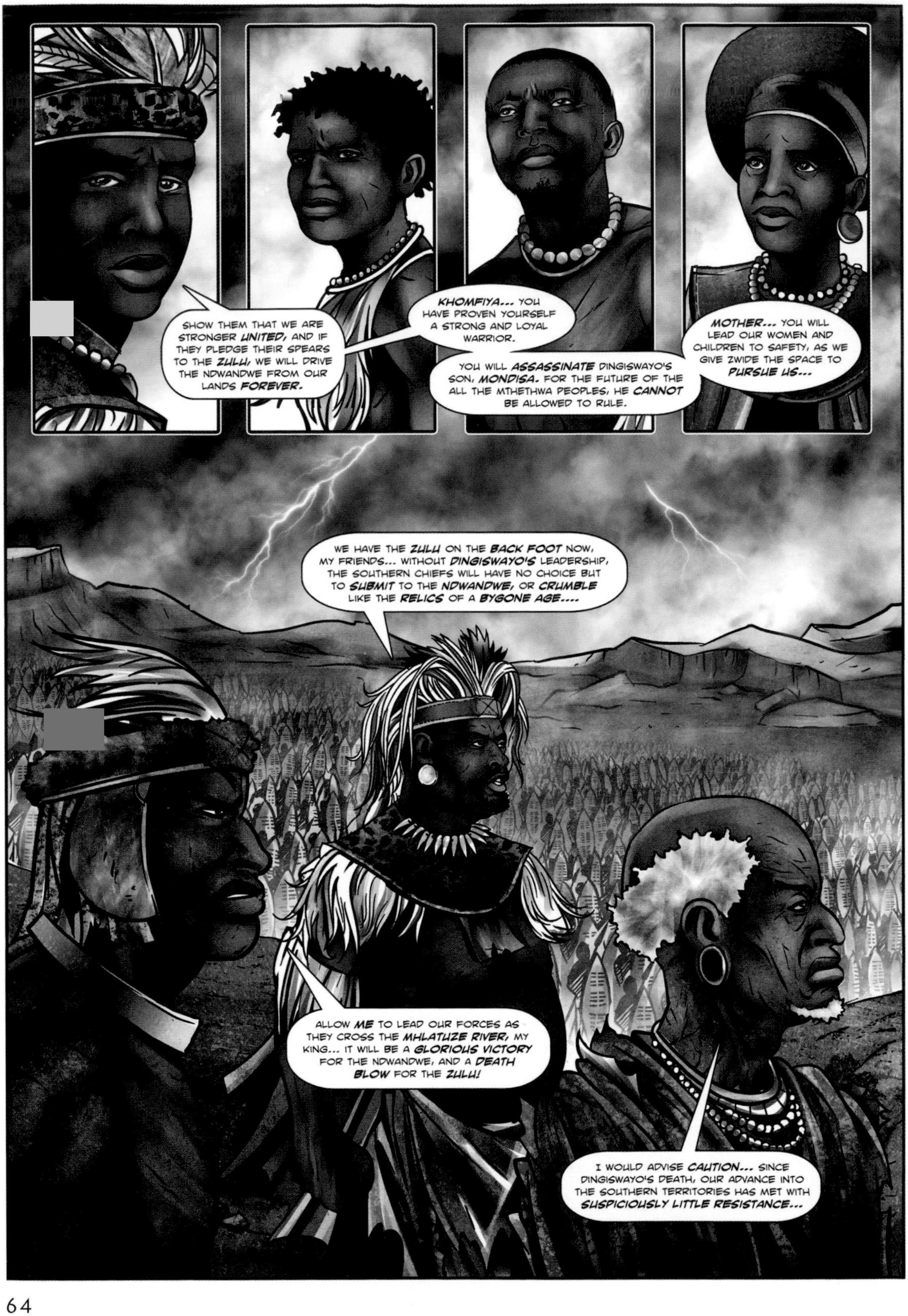
SHOW THEM THAT WE ARE STRONGER UNITED, AND IF THEY PLEDGE THEIR SPEARS TO THE ZULU, WE WILL DRIVE THE NDWANDWE FROM OUR LANDS FOREVER.
KHOMFIYA... YOU HAVE PROVEN YOURSELF A STRONG AND LOYAL WARRIOR.
YOU WILL ASSASSINATE DINGISWAYO'S SON, MONDISA. FOR THE FUTURE OF THE ALL THE MTHETHWA PEOPLES, HE CANNOT BE ALLOWED TO RULE.
MOTHER... YOU WILL LEAD OUR WOMEN AND CHILDREN TO SAFETY, AS WE GIVE ZWIDE THE SPACE TO PURSUE US...
WE HAVE THE ZULU ON THE BACK FOOT NOW, MY FRIENDS... WITHOUT DINGISWAYO'S LEADERSHIP, THE SOUTHERN CHIEFS WILL HAVE NO CHOICE BUT TO SUBMIT TO THE NDWANDWE, OR CRUMBLE LIKE THE RELICS OF A BYGONE AGE....
ALLOW ME TO LEAD OUR FORCES AS THEY CROSS THE MHLATUZE RIVER, MY KING... IT WILL BE A GLORIOUS VICTORY FOR THE NDWANDWE, AND A DEATH BLOW FOR THE ZULU!
I WOULD ADVISE CAUTION... SINCE DINGISWAYO'S DEATH, OUR ADVANCE INTO THE SOUTHERN TERRITORIES HAS MET WITH SUSPICIOUSLY LITTLE RESISTANCE...

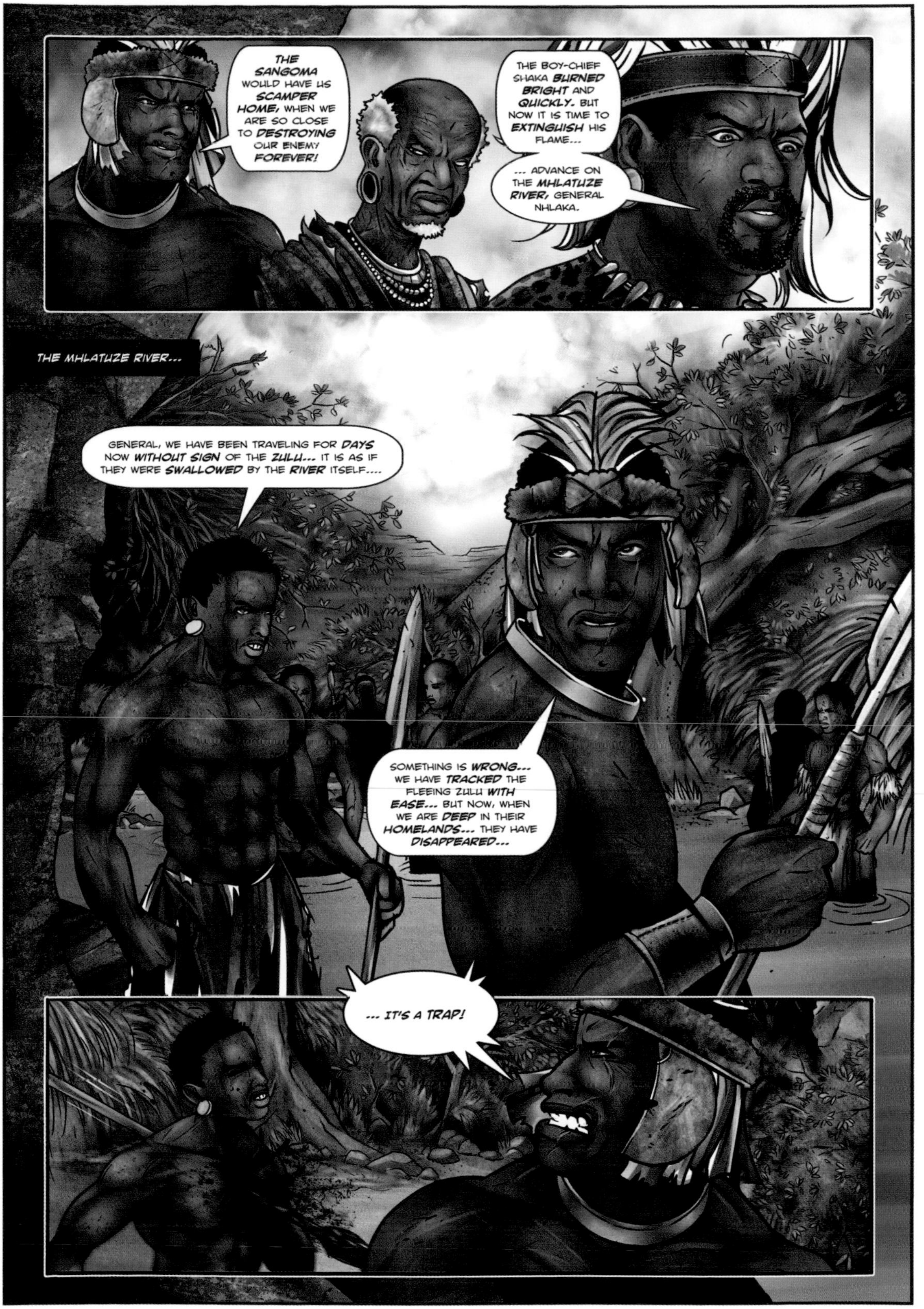
THE SANGOMA WOULD HAVE US SCAMPER HOME, WHEN WE ARE SO CLOSE TO DESTROYING OUR ENEMY FOREVER!
THE BOY-CHIEF SHAKA BURNED BRIGHT AND QUICKLY. BUT NOW IT IS TIME TO EXTINGUISH HIS FLAME...
... ADVANCE ON THE MHLATUZE RIVER, GENERAL NHLAKA.
THE MHLATUZE RIVER...
GENERAL, WE HAVE BEEN TRAVELING FOR DAYS NOW WITHOUT SIGN OF THE ZULU... IT IS AS IF THEY WERE SWALLOWED BY THE RIVER ITSELF....
SOMETHING IS WRONG... WE HAVE TRACKED THE FLEEING ZULU WITH EASE... BUT NOW, WHEN WE ARE DEEP IN THEIR HOMELANDS... THEY HAVE DISAPPEARED...
... IT'S A TRAP!

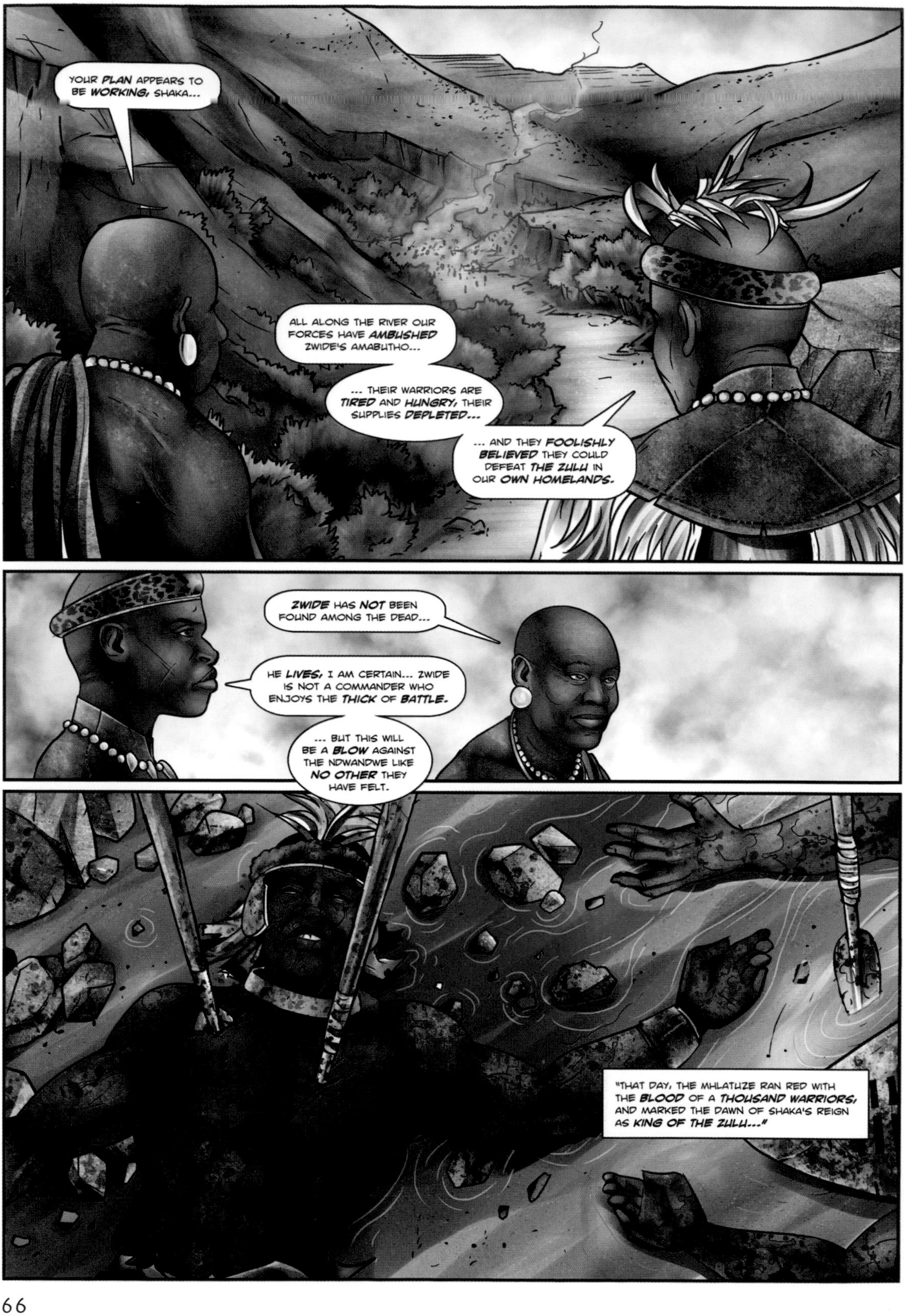
YOUR PLAN APPEARS TO BE WORKING, SHAKA...
ALL ALONG THE RIVER OUR FORCES HAVE AMBUSHED ZWIDE'S AMABUTHO...
... THEIR WARRIORS ARE TIRED AND HUNGRY, THEIR SUPPLIES DEPLETED...
... AND THEY FOOLISHLY BELIEVED THEY COULD DEFEAT THE ZULU IN OUR OWN HOMELANDS.
ZWIDE HAS NOT BEEN FOUND AMONG THE DEAD...
HE LIVES, I AM CERTAIN... ZWIDE IS NOT A COMMANDER WHO ENJOYS THE THICK OF BATTLE.
... BUT THIS WILL BE A BLOW AGAINST THE NDWANDWE LIKE NO OTHER THEY HAVE FELT.
"THAT DAY, THE MHLATUZE RAN RED WITH THE BLOOD OF A THOUSAND WARRIORS, AND MARKED THE DAWN OF SHAKA'S REIGN AS KING OF THE ZULU..."

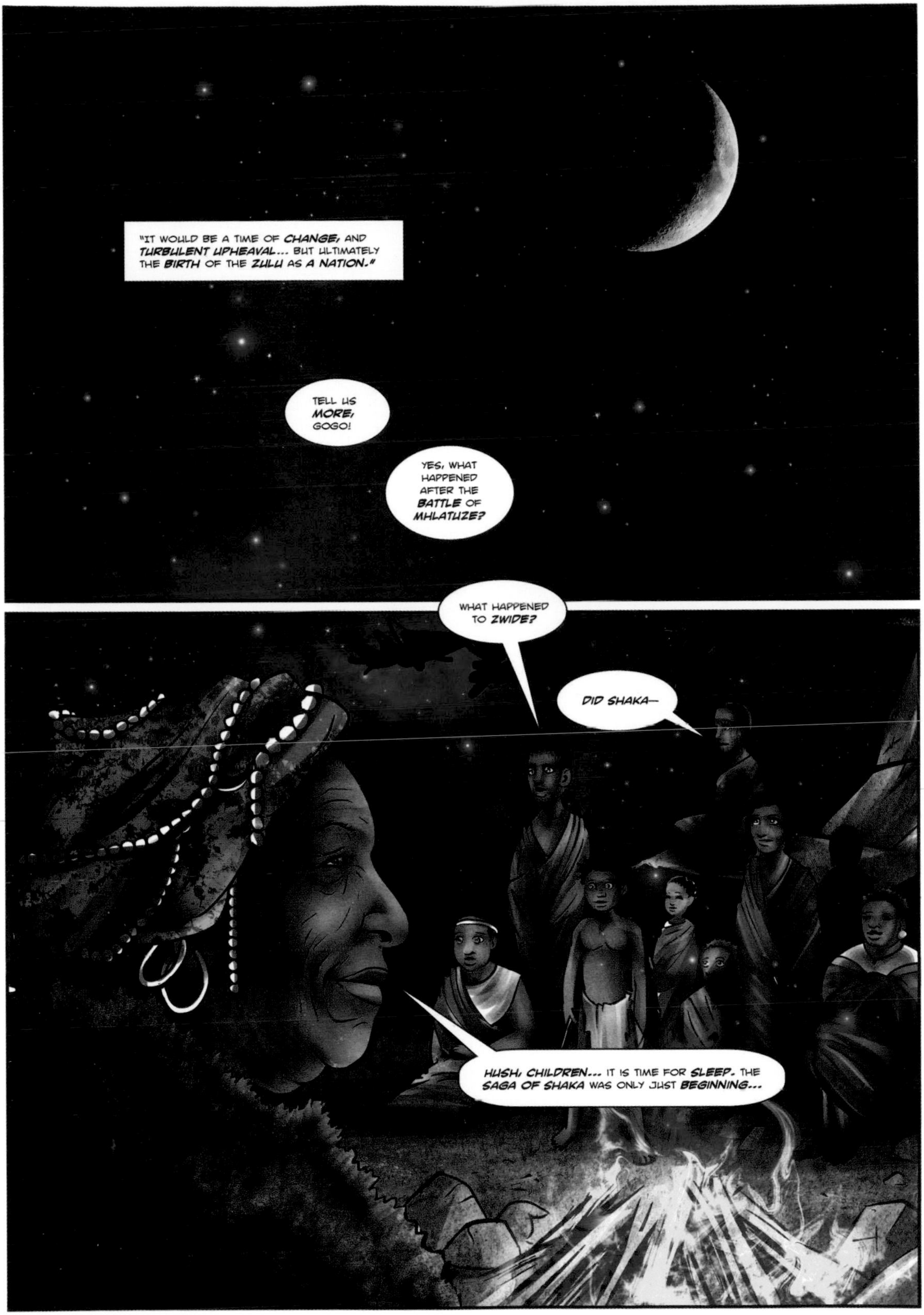
"IT WOULD BE A TIME OF CHANGE, AND TURBULENT UPHEAVAL... BUT ULTIMATELY THE BIRTH OF THE ZULU AS A NATION."
TELL US MORE, GOGO!
YES, WHAT HAPPENED AFTER THE BATTLE OF MHLATUZE?
WHAT HAPPENED TO ZWIDE?
DID SHAKA—
HUSH, CHILDREN... IT IS TIME FOR SLEEP. THE SAGA OF SHAKA WAS ONLY JUST BEGINNING...

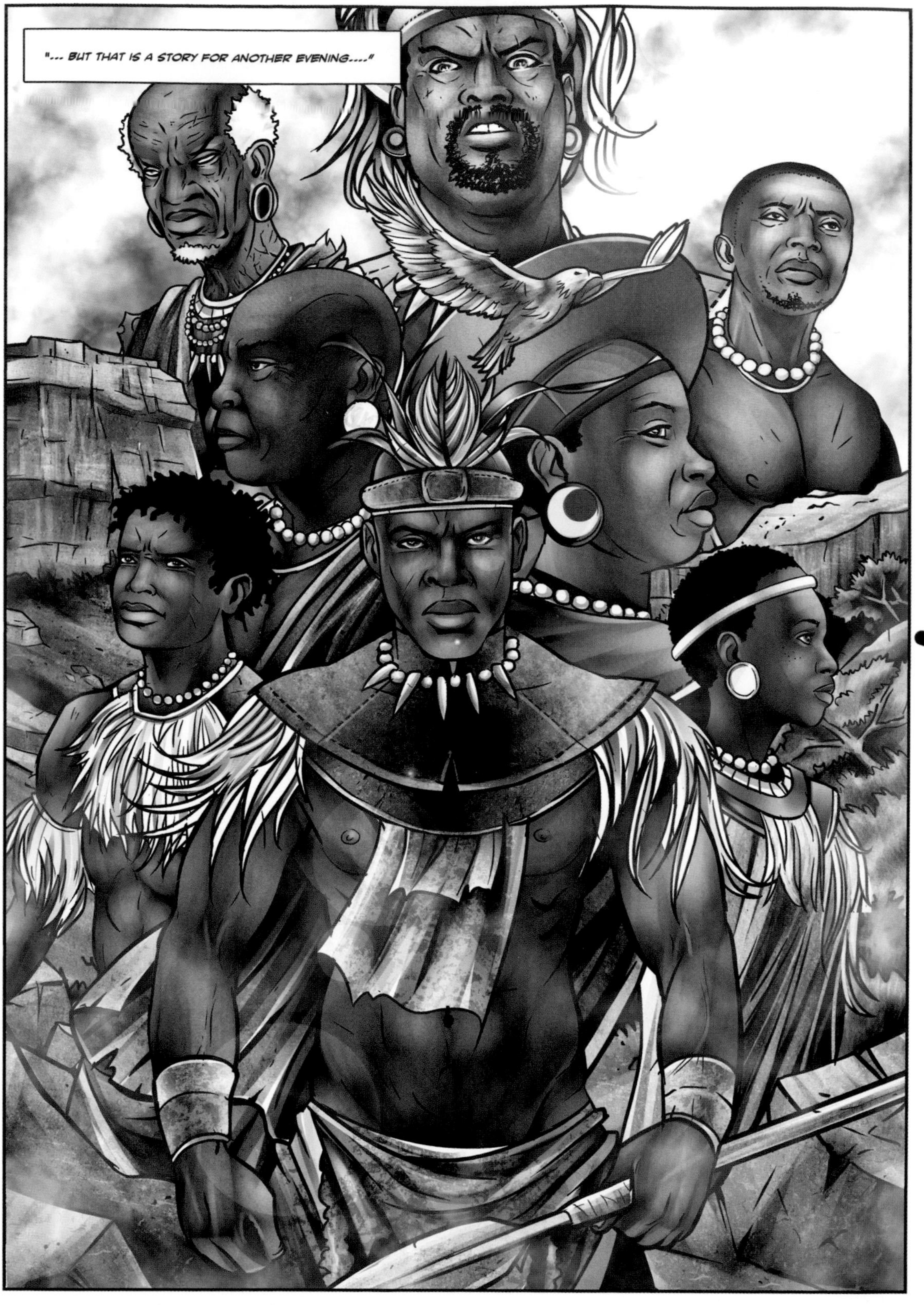
"... BUT THAT IS A STORY FOR ANOTHER EVENING...."

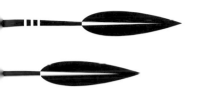

THE STORY CONTINUES

By uniting the people in a land rife with turmoil and unrest, Shaka established himself as a leader for the people. Through his tactics and political awareness, he turned the humble Zulu chiefdom into the great Kingdom of the Zulu.

AFRICA
KWAZULU-NATAL
Durban
Cape Town
SOUTH AFRICA

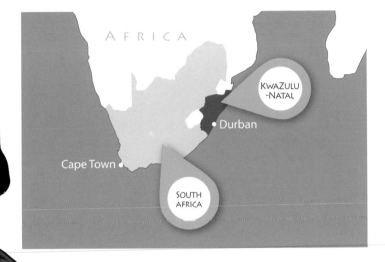

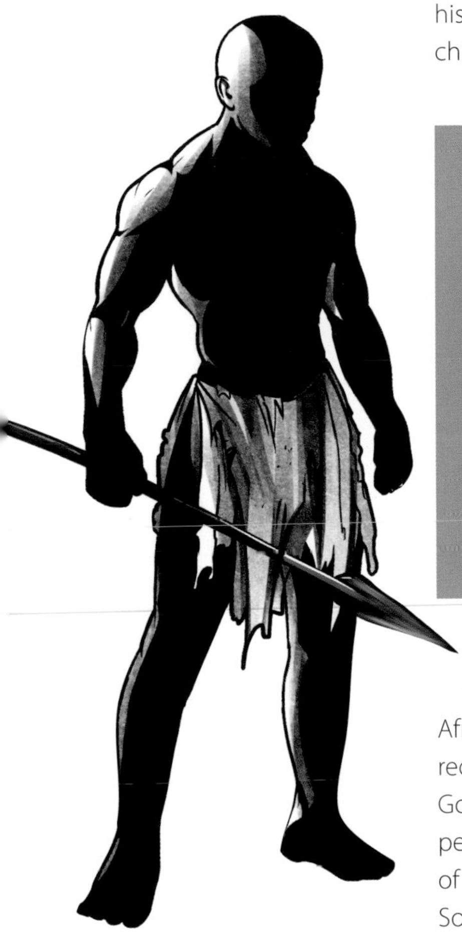

Today, Shaka's legacy lives on. The land was established as "KwaZulu" – country of the Zulu – and is now one of South Africa's nine provinces: KwaZulu-Natal. The Zulu monarchy is recognized by the state, and is currently under the rule of King Goodwill Zwelithini, a descendant of Shaka. More than 12 million people identify themselves as Zulu, constituting almost a quarter of South Africa's population, making it the largest ethnic group in South Africa.

All of this was set in motion when Shaka defeated Zwide's men, consolidating his leadership. However, this was merely the beginning of his reign, which would see more politics, warfare, and family feuds, as well as strange new pale-skinned men... and he had not seen the last of the Ndwandwe either.

How can we be sure that this story is accurate?

Shaka Rising is a "historical fiction." Based in fact, as far as possible, it is merely one "telling" of the story; but other versions do exist. Because no written form of language existed in the Zulu culture at that time, all the history of the Zulu people was retained in the telling of stories. It was not until Europeans arrived later on that details of Zulu culture were recorded in ink for the first time. These written records mostly reflect the perspectives of the European writers.

Both the oral history and the written records can prove to be sketchy. In the telling of stories, one might exaggerate, either to impress or to portray one's position in the story favorably. As these stories get passed down from generation to generation, each telling more embellished than the last, we may end up with a story bearing little resemblance to the truth. And when these stories are passed down by different people with different motives, we can end up with two completely different stories.

The written records, although not so easily altered by the "broken telephone," were often no more accurate, as they were not subject to much scrutiny, and the writers had their own agendas. The historical record about the Shaka period has left us with documents mostly authored by Europeans. In the past, these were taken at face value, as historical fact. If we inspect them more closely, however, we find that there is little evidence to support the version of the story they

AND SO SHAKA AND HIS MOTHER NANDI *LEFT* THE *ZULU* UNDER COVER OF NIGHT, THE YOUNG WARRIOR CASTING *ONE FINAL GAZE* BACK ON THE *VILLAGE* OF HIS *BIRTH*...

SEE PAGE 15

contain. Such is the case with a number of writings on Shaka. The absolute truth of what happened is, therefore, as much a legend as Shaka himself. The best one can do is look at all available records, and come to one's own conclusions of what most likely happened.

One contentious issue, for example, is that of Shaka's initial departure from the Zulu. In this version of the story, Shaka is seen to be quite old already before he leaves, and he leaves of his own accord. Others say that he and his mother were, in fact, banished by Senzangakhona while Shaka was still a child.

SEE PAGE 25

There are also aspects of Shaka's life for which very few records exist at all, and some elements of the story have been fabricated In *Shaka Rising* for the sake of exploring "what might have been." Nobuhle, for example, was made up to explore Shaka's romantic life. However, the truth is that very few accounts of Shaka's life include any sort of woman partner.

THE HISTORICAL SETTING OF SHAKA'S STORY

SEE
PAGE
2

Shaka Rising takes place in the late 18th and early 19th centuries. Shaka was born sometime in the 1780s–the date varies according to the source. The United States of America had just gained independence from British rule after the American Revolution. The French Revolution would soon follow, around the time of Shaka's childhood. Australia had just been "discovered" by the British, who would soon establish their first settlement there. The Ottoman Empire was on the decline, following a period of peace in which their military prowess had been overtaken by that of their rivals. Their influence in the trade routes between East and West became less significant with the establishment of a ship route via the Cape of Good Hope.

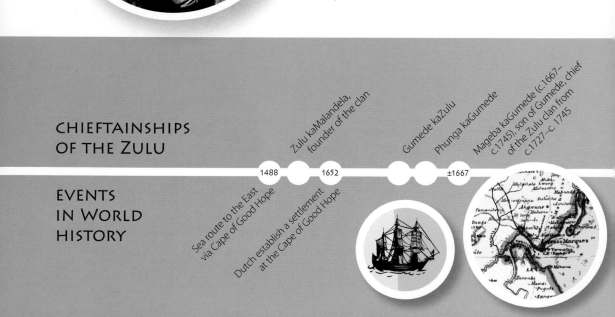

CHIEFTAINSHIPS OF THE ZULU

Zulu kaMalandela, founder of the clan

Gumede kaZulu

Phunga kaGumede

Mageba kaGumede (c.1667–c.1745), son of Gumede, chief of the Zulu clan from c.1727–c.1745

1488   1652   ±1667

EVENTS IN WORLD HISTORY

Sea route to the East via Cape of Good Hope

Dutch establish a settlement at the Cape of Good Hope

At the Cape of Good Hope (now Cape Town), the British had just taken over rule from the Dutch, and tensions were high. At Delagoa Bay (now Maputo), trading posts had been established for trade with the local peoples.

Among the items traded were things like ivory, copper, and, of course, slaves. Typically, chiefs of the area would sell their prisoners of war as slaves for a good profit. In response to an expanding slave trade, predominantly for plantation labor in South America, slavers escalated their raids on chiefdoms and villages to capture prisoners, who were then sold as slaves.

SEE PAGE 6

The Zulu were a small clan living approximately 200 km north-east of the present-day port of Durban. The time line shows the successive chiefs of the Zulu in relation to some major historical events elsewhere in the world.

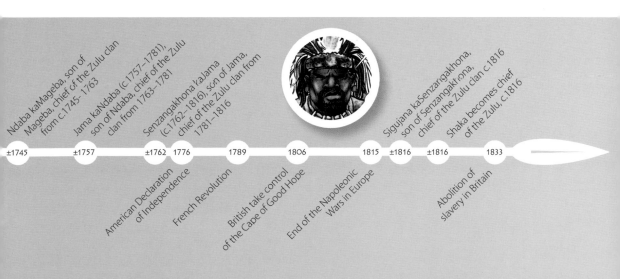

Ndaba kaMageba, son of Mageba, chief of the Zulu clan from c.1745- 1763

Jama kaNdaba (c.1757–1781), son of Ndaba, chief of the Zulu clan from 1763–1781

Senzangakhona kaJama (c.1762–1816), son of Jama, chief of the Zulu clan from 1781–1816

Sigujana kaSenzangakhona, son of Senzangakhona, chief of the Zulu clan c.1816

Shaka becomes chief of the Zulu, c.1816

±1745   ±1757   ±1762 1776   1789   1806   1815 ±1816 ±1816   1833

American Declaration of Independence

French Revolution

British take control of the Cape of Good Hope

End of the Napoleonic Wars in Europe

Abolition of slavery in Britain

Zulu Political Structures

Shaka's rise to power is often understood as a dramatic example of state-building, contrasted with the earlier, more localized, clan-based systems of power organized around homesteads of extended family groups. As chiefs began to consolidate their power in the late 18th century, they were able to demand tribute and taxes from the people they ruled through a web of social, political, and economic obligations, backed by military power. Shaka is best known for conquering neighboring chiefdoms, and uniting them into one organized kingdom under his leadership. He was able to command and extract labor from young men for both military service and building projects. In return, he offered protection and helped to resolve disputes.

SEE PAGE 59

SHAKA AS A LEADER

... THE TROOPS *CHANT* HIS *NAME* AS A *BATTLE-CRY*...

SHA-KA!

SEE PAGE 19

PATH TO LEADERSHIP

Shaka lived in a patriarchal society, in which the position of chief was handed down from father to son. But what did it take to be chosen as the son to whom the position would be passed down? Shaka was favored amongst the people to be the next chief, due to a combination of intelligence, skill as a warrior, and natural charisma.

This counted for little, however, when the mother of his half-brother Sigujana persuaded his father that Sigujana should be the next chief of the Zulu.

SEE PAGE 11

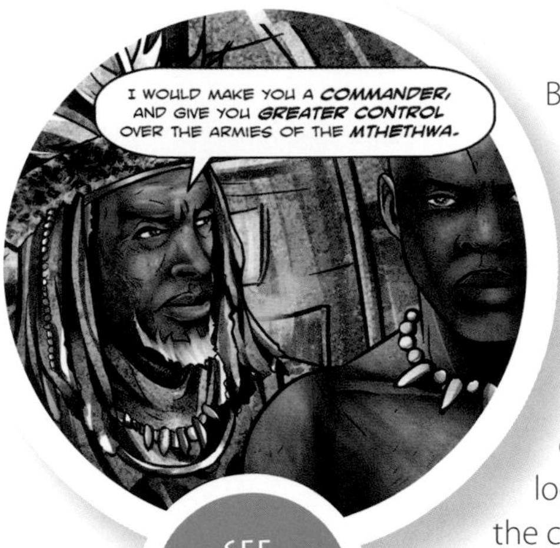
I WOULD MAKE YOU A COMMANDER, AND GIVE YOU GREATER CONTROL OVER THE ARMIES OF THE MTHETHWA.

SEE PAGE 23

But King Dingiswayo admired Shaka's traits and chose Shaka to be commander of his army.

To become chief of the Zulu, Shaka had to eliminate the competition by killing his brother. Finally, when Dingiswayo died, the paramount Mthethwa kingdom fell into disarray, and there was chaos as all the constituent clans looked for protection from the looming Ndwandwe. Shaka once again eliminated the competition, and then had to form strategic alliances to establish himself as the new king.

When we look at this story, we begin to see how important the circumstances and context are in determining new leaders. Shaka became chief partly because he was physically able to defeat his competition in battle. In modern times, this would have counted for little. His intelligence and charisma, however, would still count for a lot.

SEE PAGE 55

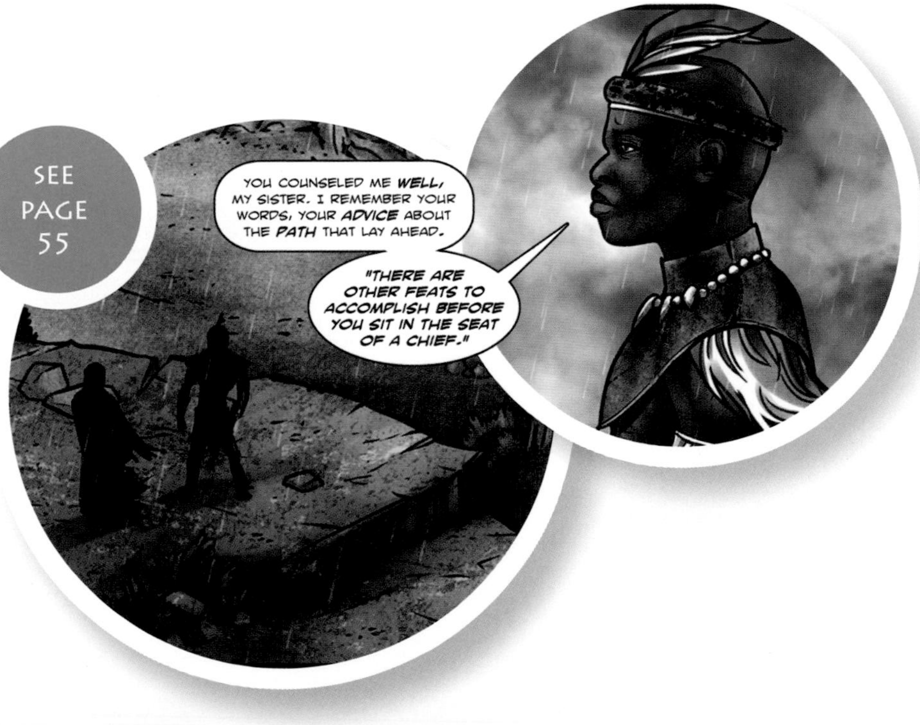
YOU COUNSELED ME WELL, MY SISTER. I REMEMBER YOUR WORDS, YOUR ADVICE ABOUT THE PATH THAT LAY AHEAD.
"THERE ARE OTHER FEATS TO ACCOMPLISH BEFORE YOU SIT IN THE SEAT OF A CHIEF."

ROLE OF A LEADER

What does it mean to be a leader? Is it social status? A job? A position of authority? Is it being the person who gets to make all the decisions? If so, why can everybody not just make their own decisions? Throughout history, humans have lived in groups, and those groups have had leaders. The Zulu had a chief. The Mthethwa had a king. Even today, we see that countries have presidents, companies have CEOs, sports teams have captains. So, what exactly is the role of a leader?

INDEED... *BLOOD* WILL SOAK THE GROUND BEFORE THE NIGHT FALLS TODAY. A *PITY*... THE SOUTHERN NATIONS WOULD BE STRONGER *UNITED,* INSTEAD OF *SPLIT* WITH *INFIGHTING.*

SEE PAGE 60

At different stages in the story, Shaka has different leadership roles to play. He leads his people into battle, forges alliances with other clans, and protects his people from the attacks of Zwide. This required tactical thinking and decisiveness, but it also required trust from the people. Being a leader carries with it authority, which is necessary when making decisions for a group. But authority can be abused. In *Shaka Rising*, we see a number of characters who are not just leaders, but rulers–each with their own characteristics and traits: Senzangakhona, Dingiswayo, Zwide, Jobe, and, of course, Shaka. Look at how each of them acts in leadership roles, and you begin to get an idea of the difference between "ruling" and "leading."

ZULU SOCIAL STRUCTURES

THE ROLE OF WOMEN

Shaka Rising took place within the setting of a patriarchal society, in which men hold power and authority over women and children. This has been a common societal construct throughout history, and south-eastern Africa was no different. This said, women in the Zulu culture were not necessarily seen as inferior. Men were the head of the household, but women were not less pivotal; everybody had their part to play.

NANDI! GO AND FETCH MORE WATER! AND TAKE SHAKA WITH YOU!

SEE PAGE 5

The Zulu culture also allowed for men to have a number of wives. Traditionally, the acquisition of more wives would be initiated by the first wife, so she could have more help with the daily chores.

The day-to-day role of women included all the general chores of running a household, including growing the crops, preparing the food, fetching the water and cleaning the house.

The most essential role of women was to raise the children: watching over them, teaching them their duties, and disciplining them. All the women of a homestead were responsible for the children.

Regardless of biological parentage, all children called each other "brother" and "sister," and all women were regarded as "Mom." The women would also be the ones to tell the children stories, an important part of Zulu culture.

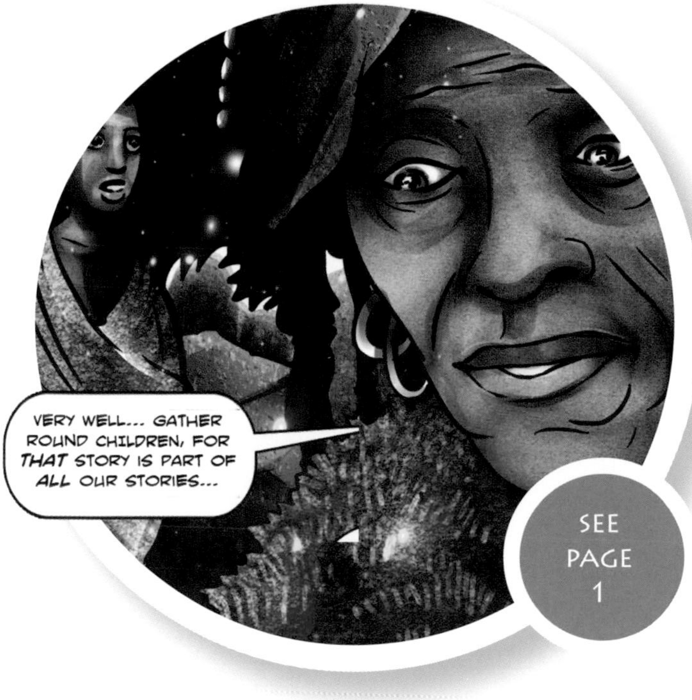
VERY WELL... GATHER ROUND CHILDREN, FOR *THAT* STORY IS PART OF *ALL* OUR STORIES...

SEE PAGE 1

Women were not without rank in society, either. The grandmother of the family was highly respected.

Other "highly ranked" women, such as the chief's wives, held considerable influence, too.

Some were even consulted as advisors, such as how Shaka consulted his mother.

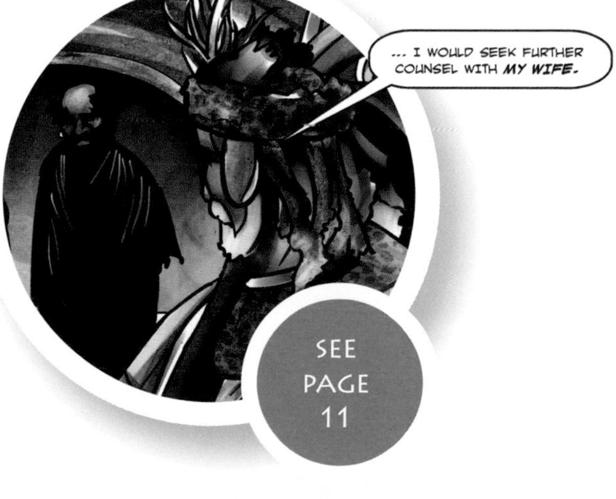
... I WOULD SEEK FURTHER COUNSEL WITH *MY WIFE.*

SEE PAGE 11

Women were also used as political devices. A chief might give his daughter or his sister to another chief as a gift to strengthen relations, or to become married into another family to create family ties and form alliances between chiefdoms.

Brothers and Sisters

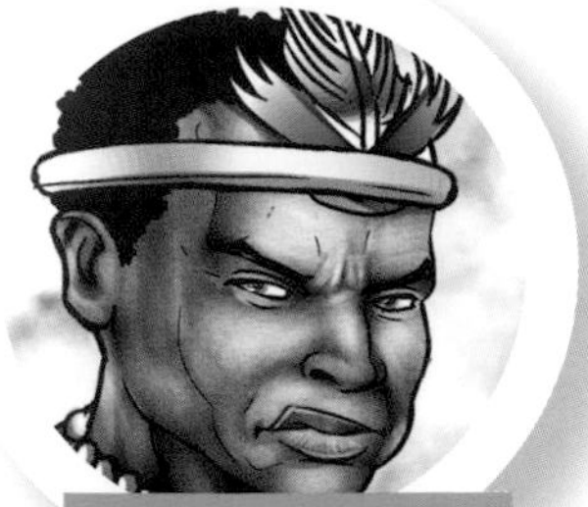

SIGUJANA
Shaka's half-brother

In this story, we meet a few of Shaka's siblings, namely Sigujana and Nomcoba, as well as Dingane and Mpande, who play an important role later in Zulu history. They were all what we today call half-siblings: they shared a father but had different mothers.

If you have any siblings, you will likely be familiar with the close bonds that you form, as well as the rivalries that occur. Shaka and Sigujana grew up together, much as brothers today would.

However, despite their history, there came a time when one brother killed the other.

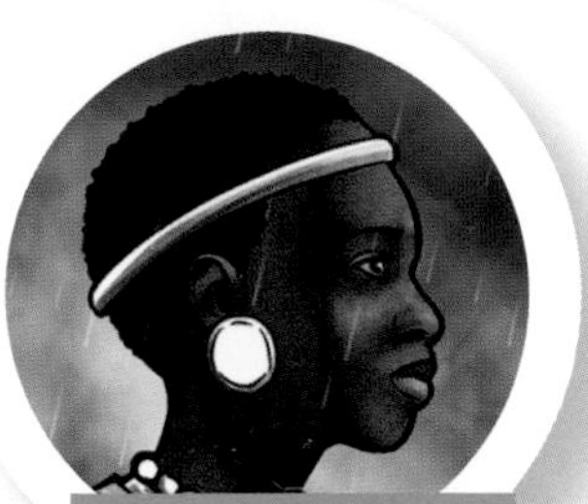

NOMCOBA
Shaka's sister

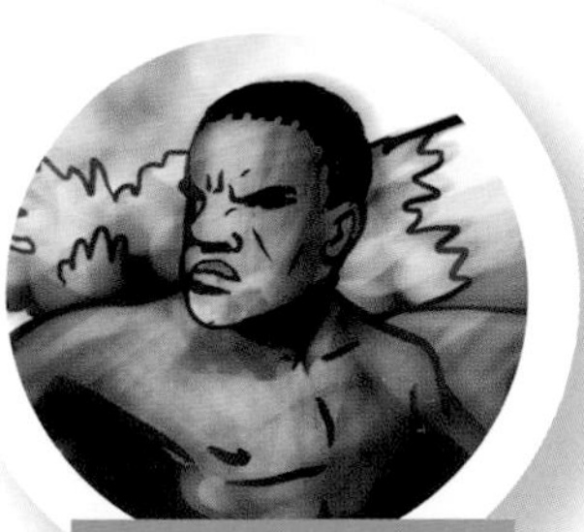

DINGANE
Shaka's half-brother

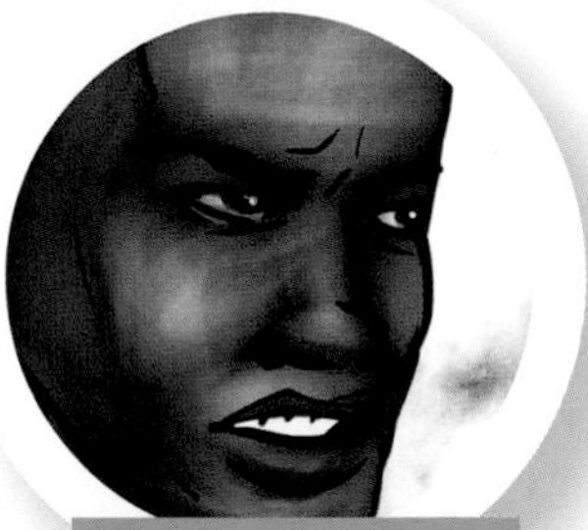

MPANDE
Shaka's half-brother

SEE PAGE 42

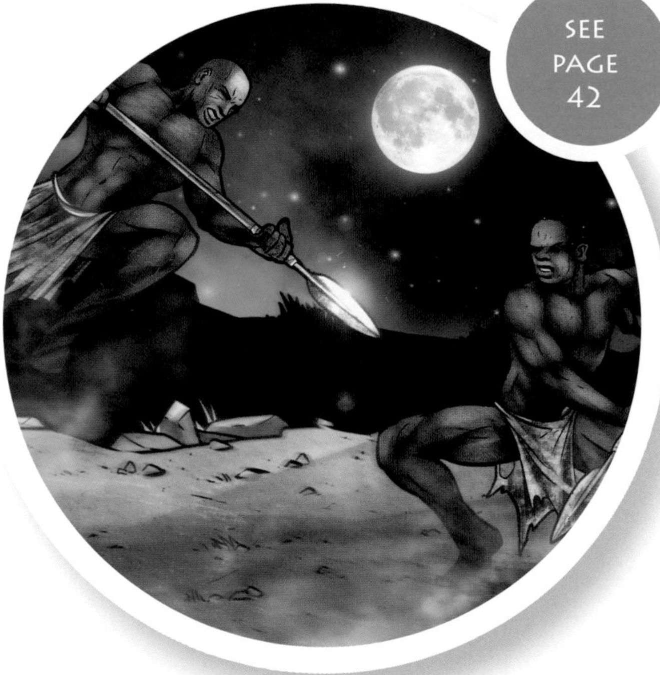

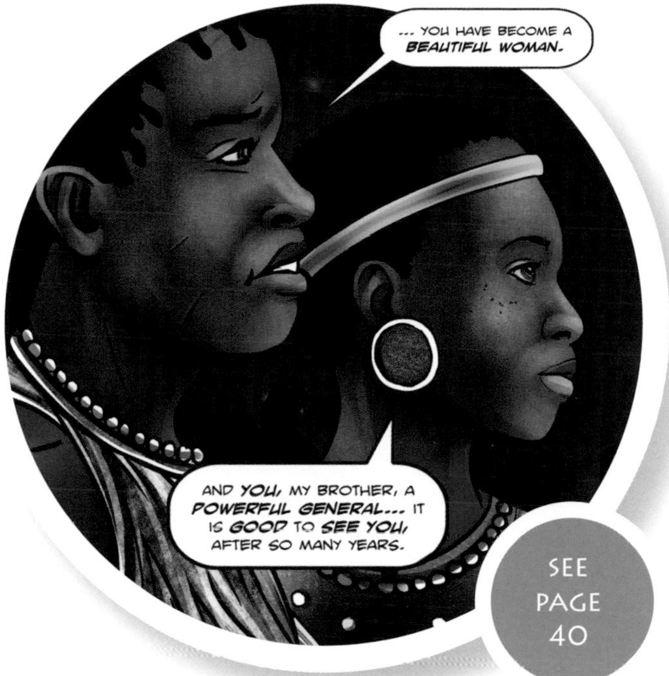
... YOU HAVE BECOME A BEAUTIFUL WOMAN.
AND YOU, MY BROTHER, A POWERFUL GENERAL... IT IS GOOD TO SEE YOU, AFTER SO MANY YEARS.

SEE PAGE 40

By today's standards, this would be seen as extreme. So, was Shaka heartless, or is this merely a reflection of the contrasting circumstances between then and now? The killing of family members sometimes occurred to eliminate rivals in an individual's path to sovereignty. Does this mean that the bond between siblings was less important than it is considered now?

Compare this with the relationship he had with Nomcoba. The two trusted and cared for each other.

Shaka did give her away to a man she did not love, but it was no easy task for him. There was still a bond between them.

SEE
PAGE
25

Families and Communities

Families would live in a ring of huts around a central cattle enclosure. The father, head of the family, would occupy the main hut at the top of the circle, and each wife and her children would have a hut either side of his. While the women tended to the daily chores, the boys would look after the livestock. Once old enough, boys would have to join an "ibutho", a regimented unit who were trained as warriors as well as performing labor tasks required by the chief. The boys would then move off to start families of their own nearby.

The exact way in which these families fitted together in political spheres is unclear. At the time of Shaka's birth, the Zulu were a small chiefdom that existed under the paramount Mthethwa kingdom. So, what did it mean to be

Zulu? Was it a question of lineage? Or living in a particular geographical location? Or having sworn allegiance to the chief? Furthermore, how did this fit into the paramount kingdom? Senzangakhona was a chief in his own right, who commanded the military power and had authority in his community. But he would answer to Dingiswayo's call as the king of the Mthethwa.

What does that say about the interactions and relationships between different chiefdoms? The only written records are those of the few European traders who passed through, subject to their Western interpretations of these different cultures and social structures. They knew little about these, especially since they were unable to understand the Zulu language. Without any reliable records, it is very difficult to say with any certainty how these communities functioned politically.

Aspects of Zulu culture

Cattle And Wealth

Cattle were the most important indication of a man's wealth and status. They were slaughtered and eaten as part of ceremonial rituals on special occasions such as weddings and funerals and also as a means to appease the ancestors in times of trauma and hardship.

Lobola ("bride-price") was a payment in cattle made by the groom to the father of the bride. Cattle were also used as currency for trading.

Cattle hide was used to make things such as garments and shields, and the horns were used as ivory.

AND WHY WOULD I NEED MORE SPEARS IN THIS SUMMER PEACETIME, BOY? IT IS CATTLE THAT HOLD VALUE THIS SEASON, AND YOU HAVE BROUGHT NONE OF THOSE TO MY VILLAGE...

SEE PAGE 10

Beads: Colorful Signals

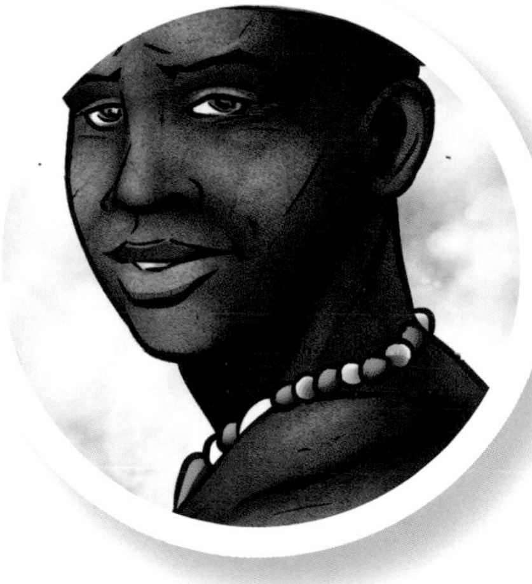

Glass beads were an integral part of Zulu culture. Different colors came to mean different things, and one would adorn oneself in an arrangement of colors for certain purposes.

A woman looking for a husband might have worn predominantly red to show fertility. She would also have worn colors chosen for her by her father to show lineage. Women also wore beads to show wealth, and they used them as a form of currency.

Headdress and Status

Commanders and chiefs would wear a crown of feathers to show authority, also usually adorned with certain beads and animal skins to show such things as lineage.

The traditional headdress of women was worn after they were married, or old enough to warrant respect.

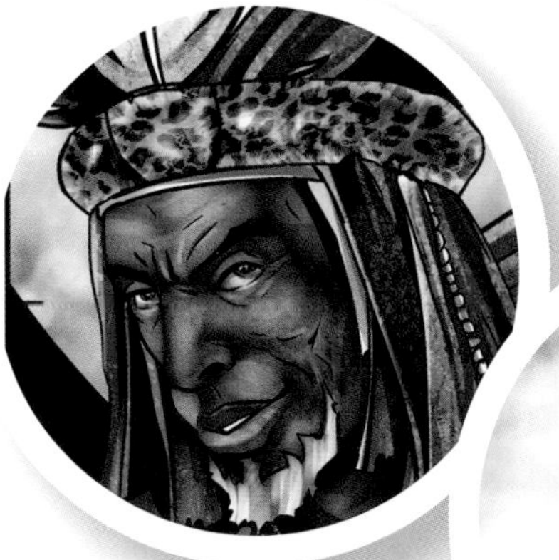

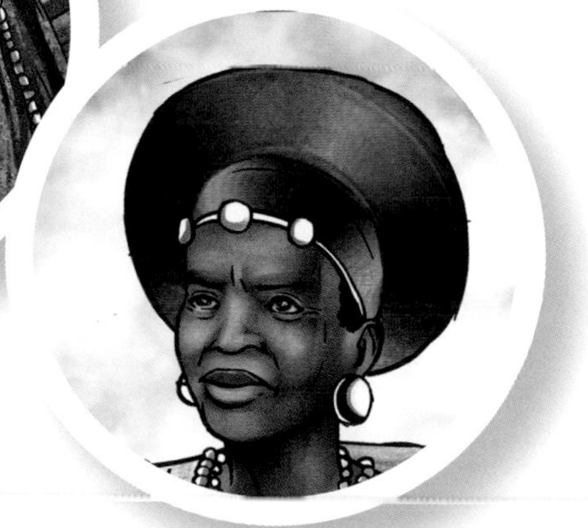

Beliefs

Belief in the supernatural was a significant aspect of Zulu culture. The ancestors of an individual and his or her clan played an important role in how Zulu people understood health and managed daily and relational conflict. Illness was broadly defined, and restoring peace within families, clans, and communities was part of managing personal and communal health. Diviners, called "izangoma," (singular: isangoma) sought help and wisdom from their ancestors and the ancestors of their patients, by throwing ceremonial bones and other objects, from which they would divine the future by the way in which they landed. Izangoma could diagnose illness, grant favorable conditions, wish ill upon another person, solve and/or create conflicts within relationships. Patients also consulted izangoma for protection from a variety of disasters such as lightning or evil spirits.

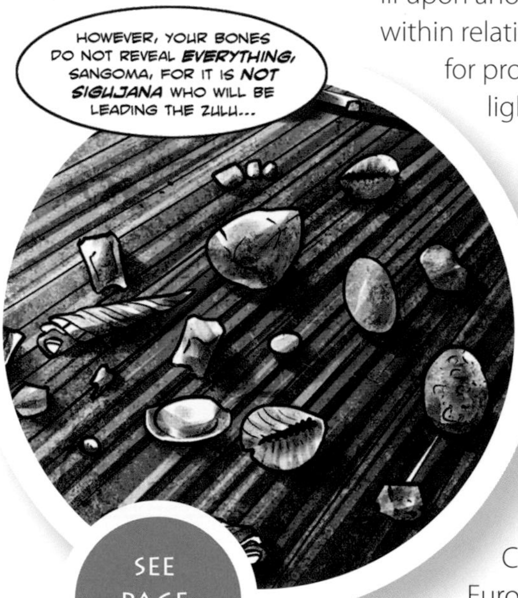
HOWEVER, YOUR BONES DO NOT REVEAL **EVERYTHING**, SANGOMA, FOR IT IS **NOT** **SIGUJANA** WHO WILL BE LEADING THE ZULU...

SEE PAGE 44

Patients further consulted herbalists, called "izinyanga." An inyanga used plants and animals to prepare medicines, known as "umuthi," to be applied to people or things for similar reasons – to cure illness, to seek health or good luck, or to curse or poison one's personal enemies. Early European travelers and settlers struggled to understand African systems of medicine, particularly as they appeared to conflict with Christian knowledge and belief systems, and European biomedical doctors and Zulu healers clashed and struggled against each other. Yet today, Zulu "traditional" healers remain an important part of a complicated medical landscape as modern Zulus continue to consult izangoma and izinyanga for a variety of illnesses and personal problems alongside their biomedical counterparts.

LANGUAGE

The dialect that was spoken at the time was common throughout most of the clans. This language has come to be known as isiZulu, the language of the Zulu.

Many Zulu words contain click sounds. In writing these are recorded by using the letters 'c', 'q', and 'x'. The sound represented by 'x' is made by sucking your tongue away from the inside of your cheek.

... YET STILL WE *SHAKE* OUR *SPEARS* AT THE *WIND!*

SEE PAGE 7

IsiZulu is a descriptive language. Words are commonly based on the sound of what they are describing. For example, there is a town called Ixopo which is close to wetlands. When you pronounce the name "Ixopo" it sounds like the hoof of a cow or horse walking in the mud.

The language also makes use of many idioms. Instead of saying, "We have no enemies to fight," one might have said, "We shake our spears at the wind."

A popular custom was that of praise poetry, which made extensive use of idioms. The praise poet would sing the chief's "praises" as a form of entertainment. Senzangakhona, for example, was called "The one who is fat even in the time of famine." To be fat during a famine would suggest he was a self-serving chief.

Shaka was said to be "The one whose fame spreads even while he is seated."

QUESTIONS AND IDEAS FOR GOING DEEPER

The way in which the material in this book is organised uses the following pattern:
- You start by reading (and viewing) the story just as it is.
- Next, there are questions and ideas to help you get a deeper understanding of what you have read.
- Finally, you think about how this applies to life as you know it (your own life, or the world in which you live).

You have read the story of Shaka as a boy and young man. In the notes and questions on pages 69-87 you have focused in more detail on particular aspects of Shaka's life The questions which follow will challenge you to think about what Shaka's life has to do with yours: What is different? What is the same? What have you learned from reading his story?

CRITICAL THINKING QUESTIONS

How accurate is this story? How do we know?
- In what other ways might the history have been skewed?
- What other instances throughout the world do you think might have been subject to fabricated history?
- Do you think it is likely that Shaka would have had a relationship with a woman, or do you think there would have been more accounts of it if he had?

The history of Shaka's time
- What was going on in other parts of the world at that time?
- How did the events at Delagoa Bay shape what happened in the story?
- How did the events in the story help shape history up to the present day?

Shaka as a leader

- To what extent do leadership positions exist today in the same social structures as in the story?
- Think about some of the leaders in society today. What are their roles and how were they chosen?
- Think about the leaders of some groups that you may have been in (sports team captain, school cheer leader, etc.). What are the roles of those positions? Were the ways in which they were chosen suitable for the positions, or could they have been done a different way?

The role of women

- Think about the role that women play in the society in which you live. In what ways is it different to that of the women in this story?
- Are the roles of women changing in our modern society? How so, and why?

Brothers and sisters

- When we compare the relationships between siblings in the story with those in our own society, what does it bring to light about the meaning we hold for the labels of "brother" and "sister"?

Social structures

- To what extent do you think this telling of the story resonates with how the characters themselves would have interpreted the situation in the context of their own culture?
- To what extent do you think the idea of a royal bloodline, such as the Zulus, was an attempt by European writers to align what they observed with their preconceived notion of monarchy, based on Western culture?

Glossary

assegai
short stabbing spear
used by Zulu warriors

Gogo
grandmother, Granny

ibutho
regiment
(plural: amabutho)

inkosi
chief

inyanga
traditional healer
(plural: izinyanga)

Iwombe
the name of one of
Dingiswayo's regiments

Nkosi
respectful way of
addressing a chief

Nkosi yami
my chief

isangoma
diviner, traditional healer
(plural: izangoma)

umuthi
traditional medicine

umuzi
homestead/settlement
(plural: imizi)

yebo
yes

PRONUNCIATION

Zulu contains some sounds which are not used in English, but it uses letters from the English alphabet to represent them.

CLICK SOUNDS: C, Q, AND X

c To make the sound of the letter 'c', suck the tip of the tongue against the palate, just behind your front teeth and then pull it away. This makes a soft click sound. It is like the sound English speakers use to show sympathy ('tsk').

q To make the sound of the letter 'q', suck the tip of the tongue against the roof of your mouth, and then pull it away suddenly. This makes a hard click sound like the sound English speakers use to imitate the sound of a horse's hoof on hard ground.

x To make the sound of the letter 'x', suck the side of the tongue against the inside of your cheek, and then pull it away suddenly. This makes a click sound like the one that English speakers use to call a horse.

English uses the sound 'th' which is not used in Zulu.

th When you see the letter combination 'th' in Zulu you can pronounce it like the English letter 't'. For example, 'Mthethwa' can be pronounced as 'Mtetwa'.